HERITAGE OF THE NORTH SEA REGION

Conservation and Interpretation

EUROPEAN COMMUNITY

European Regional
Development Fund

Interreg IIC North Sea
Region Programme

This volume and its associated conference are part of an international project on the 'Kings of the North Sea AD 250–850'. The six partners in the project are as follows:

Fries Museum, Leeuwarden, The Netherlands

Museum Het Valkhof, kunst en archeologie, Nijmegen, The Netherlands

Nordfriesisches Museum Nissenhaus, Husum, Germany

Arkeologisk Museum i Stavanger, Stavanger, Norway

Tyne and Wear Museums (Laing Art Gallery), Newcastle upon Tyne, UK

Esbjerg Museum, Esbjerg, Denmark

HERITAGE OF THE NORTH SEA REGION

Conservation and Interpretation

Edited by
L.M. Green and P.T. Bidwell

Papers presented at
the Historic Environments of the North Sea Region Conference
29–31 March 2001

DONHEAD

First published in the United Kingdom in 2002 by Donhead Publishing Ltd
Lower Coombe
Donhead St Mary
Shaftesbury
Dorset SP7 9LY
Tel. 01747 828422
www.donhead.com

ISBN 1 873394 54 3

A CIP catalogue for this book is available
from the British Library.

Printed in Great Britain by
St Edmundsbury Press, Bury St Edmunds.

This book is produced using camera copy provided by the editors.

CONTENTS

PREFACE

The conference 'Historic Environments of the North Sea Region: Conservation and Interpretation' was held at the Customs House Theatre, South Shields, from 29–31 March 2001. It formed part of an international project on the 'Kings of the North Sea AD 250–850' which was supported by the European Union's Interreg IIC North Sea Region programme and involved six partners: the Fries Museum, Leeuwarden, Netherlands, which was the lead partner; the Museum Het Valkhof, Nijmegen, Netherlands; the Nordfriesisches Museum Ludwig–Nissen–Haus, Husum, Germany; the Arkeologisk Museum i Stavanger, Norway; Tyne and Wear Museums (Laing Art Gallery), Newcastle upon Tyne, UK; and the Esbjerg Museum, Denmark.

The aims of the project were to promote and raise awareness of cultural history as well as to gain and transfer knowledge and skills in respect of:

- integrating and incorporating the results of archaeological research into international policy-making and the setting of guidelines in the fields of cultural history and town and country spatial planning
- the future international protection of monuments and archaeological and historical sites as part of town and country spatial planning, aimed at enhancing the cultural-historical and spatial qualities of the environment
- the setting-up and evaluation of international projects in the field of cultural history, in order to promote sustainable cultural-historic tourism in the North Sea region
- the organisation and management of international cultural-historic projects, techniques and design, public relations and public education, marketing and merchandising, and international fund-raising for such projects
- the development of a more permanent network focussed on cultural heritage, spatial planning and sustainable cultural tourism.

The project consisted of five components:

- an international travelling exhibition centred on trade and leadership in the Migration period and the historical heritage of the period in the landscape, which was shown at the six partner museums

- a catalogue to accompany the exhibition which was printed in five languages (the English version is *Kings of the North Sea*, edited by E. Kramer *et al.*, Den Haag, 2000)
- a programme of cultural tourism
- a seminar to evaluate the whole project but with a special focus on spatial planning and cultural tourism.

The fifth component was the South Shields conference, the papers from which are published here. The theme of the conference, which was organised by Tyne and Wear Museums Archaeology Department, was spatial planning and the historic environment from the points of view of archaeologists and spatial planning. It was attended by 80 delegates, half of whom were from the other partner countries. The papers covered a wide range of topics related to the central theme: approaches to the protection of the historic environment and its interpretation, cultural tourism, social inclusion, social and economic regeneration, and the philosophy of conservation. There were also a number of case studies, some drew on areas outside the geographical and temporal limits of the project but were able to add depth to the discussions by illustrating, for example, the problems and opportunities for interpretation of landscapes in World Heritage Sites and the role of professional engineers.

Twenty-four papers were given at the conference. Sixteen are published here and some of the remainder are intended by their authors for publication elsewhere (summaries of these papers appear at the end of this volume). One of the objectives of the conference was to produce recommendations on spatial planning and the historic environment which were presented to the project sponsors. They were the result of several periods of lively discussion during the course of the conference and are published here in full.

Linda Green
Paul Bidwell

Arbeia South Shields

ACKNOWLEDGEMENTS

On behalf of the partners of the Kings of the North Sea project, we would like to thank the European Interreg IIC North Sea Region Programme for their financial assistance. Financial contributions were also made by the local and national governments, and local organisations within each of the partner countries, to whom thanks are also given.

The partners would also like to thank Jan Walburg, Bureau Walburg, Assen, The Netherlands, who was responsible for the management of the project and the raising of the international finance.

We would like to thank the speakers who gave papers at the conference, and produced articles for inclusion in this volume. Thanks are also given to the following speakers who were unable to contribute to the volume: Magnus Fladmark, Andrew Foxon, Jan de Jong, Michael Lauenborg, Gerda Roeleveld, Flemming Thornæs, Gerald Wait and Christopher Young.

Finally, thanks to staff at Tyne & Wear Museums for their assistance, in particular Elizabeth Elliott who helped with the editing, and David Whitworth who was responsible for the design and typesetting of the volume.

LIST OF CONTRIBUTORS

Mr Geoffrey Clifton, Managing Director, Gifford and Partners, Chester, United Kingdom

Ms Astrid Dickow, Regional Planning Department, Ministry of Rural Areas, Spatial Planning, Agriculture and Tourism, Kiel, Germany

Ms Charlotte Fabech, University of Aarhus, Højbjerg, Denmark

Mr Graham Fairclough, Inspector, English Heritage, United Kingdom

Dr Sally M Foster, Senior Inspector of Ancient Monuments, Historic Scotland, United Kingdom

Ministerialrat Ernst Hansen, Head of Division of Interstate and Interregional Planning, Ministry of Rural Areas, Spatial Planning, Agriculture and Tourism-Planning Group, Kiel, Germany

Mr Henrik Jarl Hansen, Head of the National Record of Sites and Monuments, National Museum, DKC, Copenhagen, Denmark

Mr Colin Haylock, School of Architecture, Planning and Landscape, University of Newcastle upon Tyne, Newcastle upon Tyne, United Kingdom

Mr David Heslop, County Archaeologist, Tyne and Wear, United Kingdom

Dr philos Anne-Sophie Hygen, Advicer in conservation and management of pre-Reformation cultural heritage sites and monuments, Directorate for Cultural Heritage, Oslo, Norway

Mr Dré van Marrewijk, Ministry of Agriculture, Nature Management and Fisheries, Directorate North, Groningen, The Netherlands

Priv Doz Dr Dirk Meier, Forschungs- und Technologiezentrum Westküste, Arbeitsgruppe Küstenarchäologie, Büsum, Germany

Mr Carsten Paludan-Müller, Head of Cultural Heritage Division, Ministry of Environment and Energy, National Forest and Nature Agency, Copenhagen, Denmark

Prof Ulf Näsman, Department of Prehistoric Archaeology, University of Aarhus, Højbjerg, Denmark

Mr Jakob Kieffer-Olsen, Director, Museet Ribes Vikinger, Ribe, Denmark

Mr Geir Sør-Reime, Senior Advisory Officer, Rogaland County Council, Stavanger, Norway

Ms Jytte Ringtved, University of Aarhus, Højbjerg, Denmark

Mr Erling Sonne, Architect, Ribe Kommune, Teknisk Forvaltning, Ribe, Denmark

Dr John Williams, Head of Heritage Conservation, Directorate of Strategic Planning, Kent County Council, Kent, United Kingdom

1

NORWEGIAN NATIONAL APPROACH TO SPATIAL PLANNING AND THE HISTORIC ENVIRONMENT

Geir Sør-Reime

Inspired by British and Continental ideas, interest in the preservation of historic monuments arose from the beginning of the nineteenth century in Norway. The rescue of the medieval stave churches, at that time being demolished due to the need for larger churches created by the unification of congregations, was the first priority of these pioneer conservationists. Simultaneously, interest in archaeological sites rose. The quest for historic, national identity was an important element in the struggle for complete national independence during the nineteenth century. The first national legislation listing ancient monuments automatically came into force in 1905, upon national independence from Sweden. Legislation for the listing of buildings came into force in 1920. These acts concentrated on single monuments and sites; in fact, in several instances even parts of buildings were listed.

Only during the 1970s, with the establishment of a separate Ministry of the Environment and the introduction of legislation for nature conservation, were the ideas of the conservation of larger areas or entities introduced. A direct link between conservation and planning legislation was established at the same time. But it was not until early 1990 that legislation for the protection of larger cultural heritage areas was introduced into the Heritage Act. Simultaneously, the regional authorities became directly responsible for the integration of the historic environment into spatial planning. After 10 years of this integrated approach, much still remains to be done, but much has also been achieved.

FROM SINGLE MONUMENTS TO LANDSCAPE FEATURES

The first Acts dealing with the listing of archaeological and architectural heritage in Norway were, as already mentioned, concerned with the valuable historical monuments themselves and had no provisions to protect their environment or to safeguard their landscape impact. The 1905 Act on the listing and protection of ancient monuments declared that all prehistoric and medieval monuments known or not yet uncovered/discovered were automatically listed.

The first step towards protection of the landscape impact of archaeological sites came in 1951, when the 1905 Act on listing and protection of ancient monuments was revised. The new paragraph 4 said that the Ministry could list 'as large an area around a listed monument as is felt necessary to protect it and its landscape impact'. The same paragraph also repeated a 1921 legal basis for the Ministry to demand that buildings and other constructions which disturbed the landscape impact should be demolished, and also the provisions for Ministerial approval of new buildings and constructions close to ancient monuments.

The acts on the listing of archaeological and architectural heritage were merged into the single Cultural Heritage Act in 1978. This Act went into force in 1979, and, with several amendments, is still in force. The old paragraph 4 of the 1905 Act was split into two. A new paragraph 6 made provisions for a so-called 'security zone': that is, an extended zone of listing around automatically listed archaeological sites to protect them from disturbances. Although it says in the Act that this zone should be individually delimited for each site, in practice the general rule of 5 m from the visible boundary of the monument or site has been adopted for almost all sites. In fact, in our county no individual delimitation has been set for any site.

Probably more important was a new paragraph 21 (currently paragraph 19), which was concerned with the protection of the area around a protected monument or site. The paragraph states that:

> The Ministry may protect an area around a protected monument or site or a ship find ... in so far as this is necessary to preserve the effect of the monument etc. in the environment or to protect scientific interests associated with it.

AREA PROTECTION AND SPATIAL PLANNING PRACTICE PRIOR TO 1990

It is one thing to have a legal basis for listing areas to safeguard the landscape impact of ancient monuments and provisions to prevent buildings etc. being erected close to such monuments. The test is, of course, is whether these provisions are actively utilised by the authorities.

If we look first at the 1921 Act which aimed to protect listed monuments etc. from visual disturbance by new buildings and constructions, it is safe to say that it had very little impact. It was not until the 1951 Act that a system was introduced whereby area plans (area planning guidelines), site briefs, and applications for new buildings, had to be sent for checking and approval to the competent authorities as part of the ordinary assessment process.

Again, the implementation of these regulations was slow in practice and the system did not begin to function adequately until the early 1970s. Although the 1965 Buildings Act had introduced provisions for areas to be defined as protected areas in area plans, little use of these provisions can be recorded prior to the 1970s.

The major result of these provisions, especially for the period between 1970 and 1985, was a huge increase in large-scale archaeological investigations and excavations and subsequently, an enormous increase in the academic base knowledge of Norwegian prehistory. When the archaeological authorities, at that time the five archaeological museums, started to realise the potential of the provisions of the Acts, they started demanding large-scale inventories of areas under planning. This resulted in a number of excavation projects, mainly on Stone Age sites. In fact, it dramatically increased the information base on this period of our prehistory. Later, from about 1980, archaeologists also realised that hidden under the surface they could find traces of Bronze Age and Iron Age settlements, such as post-holes, wall foundations and fire-places from houses.

So the major impact of these conservation regulations was a race for excavations. Instead of protecting monuments, the Act was used as a vehicle to finance a veritable boom in the removal of archaeological evidence from the soil.

This development was, of course, furthered by the provisions of the Act which said that the planner or developer should pay all costs relating to the archaeological investigation of planning areas or development sites.

To a minor extent from the mid-1980s, the archaeological authorities started to demand that areas be set aside for the protection of listed sites in area plans and site briefs, based on the Building Act provisions. The main difference between extended listing based on the Ancient Monuments Act and the provisions in the Building Act is that the latter is not a legal listing, but a protective measure taken by the planning authority (usually the local council) and can be revoked by the same body. The practical implications of the two ways of protection can be identical.

Based on their role according to the Building Act, the archaeological museums in several instances demanded that a larger area surrounding listed monuments should be defined as a protection area in area plans and site briefs. Gradually, the number of such protection areas surrounding listed sites has grown to such an extent that no-one knows how many areas exist and where they are.

AN ABRUPT ATTEMPT – THE NATIONAL HERITAGE INSPECTOR

Based on the realisation that the provisions of the 1951 Act for listing larger areas surrounding listed monuments had not been utilised to any extent, the Norwegian Culture Council appointed a committee of archaeologists in 1965 to look into measures to safeguard the most precious archaeological sites of Norway. The committee states in their report that in practice the then current Act (of 1951) had no effective provisions to safeguard even the most spectacular archaeological sites. On the contrary, new buildings or constructions had recently surrounded a number of high-class sites, often disturbing or destroying the landscape impact of these monuments. The committee, therefore, came up with the suggestion that 233 sites and their environs should be protected through an outright purchase of the surrounding land.

Based on the recommendations of the committee, the post of National Heritage Inspector was set up and funds were made available for the purchase of land. The progress of the purchasing scheme was slow, as it turned out that landowners would not sell outright but demanded concessions such as the right to continue grazing on the land. During the few years that the scheme was in force, only a small number of sites were protected in this way. The impressive row of majestic Bronze Age mounds at Reheia on Karmøy was the only site purchased in our county (Figure 1), although 37 sites had been proposed in the plan.

Taking the lack of co-operation between heritage and planning authorities prior to 1990 into account, it is probably not surprising that the first local plan for the whole municipality of Karmøy, where Reheia is situated, did not show the purchased area as a protected area. The area was only shown as a protected area on the plan, after the Museum of Archaeology, Stavanger raised objections (according to the Planning and Building Act of 1985, paragraphs 20–5). It must be added that the municipal authorities later took their responsibilities seriously. As part of a Raphael-funded project called 'European Cultural Paths', the area was given a complete face-lift. Old posts were taken down, a new access road with parking area was constructed, and new signboards were put up. In addition, a guide brochure was produced.

This all happened in close co-operation with the County Council (responsible for the care of ancient monuments) and the Museum of Archaeology, Stavanger (the responsible authority for giving permission for undertakings

Figure 1 Reheia. The huge Guttorm's Mound dating from the Bronze Age, part of a row of six surviving majestic mounds. The mounds with their surrounding area were bought by the Government in the 1960s as part of a plan to safeguard the most important archaeological sites of Norway.

in protected areas, and the representative of both the owner and National Government).

REGIONALISATION OF CULTURAL HERITAGE ADMINISTRATION IN 1990

Prior to 1990, the five archaeological museums in Norway had the sole responsibility for prehistoric monuments according to the Act. The National Board of Antiquities only had limited responsibilities, primarily for listed buildings and for medieval monuments. This system was radically changed in 1990. On the one hand, the National Board of Antiquities became a Directorate responsible for the entire cultural heritage administration and on the other, much of the implementation of the Act was delegated to the County Councils instead of the archaeological museums. The museums, however, still retained the right to remove listings and to carry out excavations. The purpose of this change to the system was partly to make decision-making relating to the Cultural Heritage Act more democratic.

The County Councils already had the right to veto municipal area plans. This right was now linked to similar provisions in the Cultural Heritage Act. It became mandatory for municipal authorities to send their area plans relating to cultural heritage to the County Council. Every County Council was given an Archaeological and a Building Conservation Officer by the Government.

No doubt, this re-organisation resulted in much more effort being spent on scrutinising local plans, area plans and site briefs with regard to their implications for the cultural heritage. Archaeologists would inspect the areas in question more frequently than before. It was also important that the County Archaeologists had no power or right to carry out excavations, but had the preservation of the archaeological heritage as their prime goal. As a result, demands for the conservation of sites and monuments became more frequent through the planning process. Plans often had to be altered to accommodate these demands. Naturally, conflicts arose, but they were often solved through dialogue between the antiquarian authorities and the local councils.

Often demands came for the area surrounding a listed site or monument to be set aside as a preservation area according to the Planning and Building Act. From 1990 onwards, there was a dramatic rise in the number of listed sites and monuments gaining increased environmental protection through the planning process.

THE NEW INITIATIVE, PARAGRAPH 20 IN THE CULTURAL HERITAGE ACT

One of the first real national initiatives to incorporate larger contiguous cultural-historic environs into the preservation and planning acts, was the inclusion of cultural environment (as it is called in the official translation of the Cultural Heritage Act of 1978 with later amendments) into the Act in 1992. At the same time, in October 1992 there came a ministerial circular concerning the relationship between cultural heritage and planning based upon the Planning and Building Act (of 1985). It established the duties of municipalities and County Councils in order to implement the provisions of the Cultural Heritage Act into the planning processes based on the Planning and Building Act. It is important to note that a County Council can raise legal objections to a local plan based upon cultural-historic values even if there are no listed buildings or areas in the plan area.

Returning for a while to the Cultural Heritage Act, the new paragraph 20 introduced in 1992 says 'A cultural environment may be protected by the King in order to preserve its cultural-historic value.'

In August 1992, the National Board of Antiquities started a project to look into the potential of, and problems relating to, the new provisions for cultural environment listing provided by the 1992 amendments.

The task of the project was two-fold. In addition to coming up with proposals relating to the evaluation of cultural environments and their cultural-historic values, the project also aimed to define more clearly which monuments and sites were of national importance. Leaving the latter problem here, the main aim was to come up with criteria for the listing of cultural environments according to the new paragraph 20.

THE RESULTS OF THE 1992 PROJECT GROUP ON THE LISTING OF CULTURAL ENVIRONMENTS

Paragraph 20 was intended to give a legal basis for the listing of larger contiguous areas of cultural-historic interest. The term 'cultural environments' is meant to include cultural landscapes, cityscapes, etc. where cultural remains are part of a larger whole or context. It is explicitly stated that a cultural environment may be listed even if no single object within the context itself would have been eligible for listing.

The project tried to define 'cultural environment' also from an academic angle, and came to the conclusion that it is a combination of physical, social and historic qualities relating to a given landscape. It came up with a set of preliminary criteria for the evaluation of cultural environments. It is vital to underline that these were sketchy and had to be tested against concrete cases.

CASES: THE FIRST CULTURAL ENVIRONMENT LISTINGS

Although the legal basis for the listing of cultural environments was already available in 1992, and the first theoretical attempts at defining and delimiting them were also made in this year, it proved to be a long and difficult process before the first cultural environments listings were made.

To date, proposals for 12 cultural environment listings have been made in Norway. Three of these have been withdrawn, three have been passed and five are still under consideration. One area has been transferred to protection under the Natural Conservation Act.

In Rogaland County we have experienced this process from two different angles. Firstly, the area surrounding Norway's only preserved monastery at Utstein, one of our cultural environments, was one of two such environments selected by the Ministry of the Environment and the National Board of Antiquities as a test case for the new type of listing. Secondly, we started the process of listing the old small town of Sogndalstrand, on our own, according to the same provisions. The two processes have probably mutually influenced each other, and in the end, they were both managed as one process by the Ministry.

The core element in this area is Utstein Monastery, the best-preserved monastery in Norway (Figure 2).

Listing of this area had been proposed as early as 1978. At that time, listing according to the Natural Conservation Act was intended. For various reasons, however, the progress of the listing proposal was slow, and when, in 1992, the Cultural Heritage Act provided for the listing of the cultural environments, it was decided to apply for that. In 1994, the first formal proposal for listing of the area according to the new act was put forward by the Ministry of Environment. The listed area comprised of 2,500,000 sq m. The motivation for the listing, in addition to the monastery itself, was composed of several elements:

- the location of the monastery in a characteristic and beautiful landscape, dominated by grazing lands
- the still visible traces of agricultural cultivation throughout the ages
- the large number of ancient monuments which includes the remains of prehistoric fences, farm houses, clearing mounds, and a number of burial mounds

Figure 2 Utstein monastery. The monastery itself is almost covered by trees in the centre of the picture. The monastery and the cultural landscape surrounding it were listed as a cultural environment on 17 December 1999.

- current agricultural activity contributes to the maintenance of a varied and well managed farm landscape.

In the listing order it is stated that the purpose of the listing is:

> to protect and maintain a special and grazing-dominated cultural environment by Utstein Monastery, with high national qualities in regard to the special cultural-historic landscape and agricultural elements that contribute to giving the area its specific characteristics. This incorporates specific elements of the cultural environment and the landscape, important single elements and the connection between the elements.

The monastery, as a medieval building, was automatically listed so it was the surrounding landscape that came into focus when the environment listing process started. The main objective of the listing is, therefore, to safeguard the character of the landscape surrounding the monastery. After a long process involving local farmers and the local and regional authorities, the listing of the area was announced through an Order in Council on 17 December 1999.

It has been crucial to incorporate the listing of the cultural environment area into the local and regional area plans. The area is shown as a protected area in the current municipal area plan for the municipality of Rennesøy. It is also incorporated into the County Council's strategic plan for city development around Stavanger. Due to the high number of agricultural, historical and biological values of a large area surrounding the listed area, city development here is not recommended in the plan.

ANOTHER CASE: THE SMALL TOWN OF SOGNDALSTRAND

Sogndalstrand was once an important port south of Stavanger with its own customs house, several merchants and a large merchant fleet. Established as a township in the seventeenth century, it received privileges as a township in 1798. In the twentieth century its importance diminished, and in 1944, during the German occupation, the town council was abolished. The town's independence was not restored after liberation, and most economic activity moved to the centre of the surrounding rural municipality. The good thing about this, of course, is that the town has remained relatively unchanged since the late nineteenth century (Figure 3), and the urban cultural landscape has been preserved to a large degree. The citizens fed their animals from the grazing lands surrounding the town, and some even had storage barns in these lands.

Unfortunately, during the 1960s and 1970s, a number of new houses were built just outside the old town. In the early 1990s, plans for large-scale

Figure 3 Sogndalstrand. Row of old warehouses along the river mouth. The County Council has proposed a cultural environment listing for the town and its surrounding area. The final listing proposal was sent for Government approval on 5 October 2000.

development of housing were presented. Rogaland County Council took the opportunity offered by the new legislation, and announced a temporary listing pending final listing approval on 3 May 1994. Before issuing the provisional listing order, the County Council consulted both the Municipal Council and the National Board of Antiquities. Just after the issuing of the order, there was a public meeting in the town which presented it to the public. Thereafter, a long process began which included meetings and discussions, in order to determine the boundaries, regulations, etc. for the final listing. A formal listing proposal was sent to all parties in February 1999. After it had been approved by the regional and local authorities, the proposal was sent for Government approval on 5 October 2000. Approval is still pending, but the work on a management plan has already started.

It can already be concluded that the focus on preservation caused by the listing proposal has had a number of positive effects. The debate has resulted in an increase in visitor numbers, which has led to the re-opening of a shop. A hotel has also opened, and is expanding its business to neighbouring houses. Now local people can live from the preservation, so to speak.

CONCLUSION

In conclusion, I have to admit that although legal provisions have existed for quite a number of years, the integration of historic environments into the spatial planning processes has been slow in Norway. During the last decade, National, regional and local authorities have addressed this problem seriously, and we are currently witnessing major improvements in this area.

References

Kulturseksjonen, Rogaland fylkeskommune, *Forvaltningsplan for Utstein kulturmiljø, Rennesøy kommune, arbeidsdokument pr.16.01.01* (restricted), 2001.

Miljøverndepartmentet, *Cultural Heritage Act,* Oslo, (Circulars from Ministry of the Environment series) T-1342, 2000.

Latest version available on http://odin.dep.no/md/engelsk/

Earlier versions referred to exist only in Norwegian: Miljøverndepartmenetet, *Rundskriv, nye forskrifter til kulturminneloven om faglig ansvarsfordeling mv. - delegasjon,* (T-6/89), 1989. Miljøverndepartmenetet, *Lov om kulturminner,* (T-971), 1992.

Norsk Kulturråd, *Innstilling fra utvalget for sikring av høyt prioriterte fornminner,* 1967.

Riksantikvaren , *Nasjonale verdier og vern av kulturmiljøer,* Riksantikvarens notater 1–1993, 1993.

Stavanger Museum, Lov om fortidsminner, 1951.

Stortinget, *Plan- og bygningslov (Planning and Building Act),* Grøndahl Dreyer Lovdata, 1997.

2

SPATIAL PLANNING IN GERMANY AND SCHLESWIG–HOLSTEIN

Astrid Dickow

This paper provides an overview of spatial planning systems in Germany at federal and regional levels, focussing on Schleswig–Holstein. The general theme is continued in Chapter 3, where Ernst Hansen discusses the inclusion of cultural heritage in regional planning.

Above the several levels of planning in Germany is the European level with its European regional development concept (Figure 1). The federal level in Germany has a frame competence in the field of spatial planning. This means that the Federation itself has no binding national plan. The Federal Ministry for Spatial Planning, however, has produced a set of guidelines (Federal Regional Planning Act, last published 18 August 1997), which are fundamental to spatial planning in Germany. The Act obliges the states to draw up regional plans in which specifications are made about the desired settlement structure, open space structure and infrastructure locations and routes.

Due to the federal nature of Germany, each state has a slightly different approach to spatial planning and the content of regional plans. In Schleswig–Holstein (Figure 2), since the last elections, the Regional Planning Department forms part of the Ministry of Rural Areas, Regional Planning, Agriculture and Tourism. The department is responsible for both state and regional planning, as there is no middle administration level in Schleswig–Holstein. In other states there is a middle level with administrative districts, each consisting of a couple of counties. In Schleswig–Holstein, the Regional Planning Department draws up a state regional plan and regional plans for each of the five regions which make up the state. A structure, therefore, exists which unites counties for this purpose, but there is no administration on this level. The plans are valid for 15 years so the regional plans have to take into account the aims of the state regional plan. In doing so, the state regional planning authority focuses on the main goals rather than the formulation of

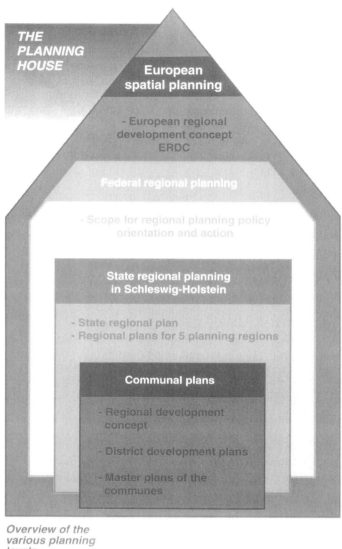

THE
PLANNING
HOUSE

European
spatial planning

- European regional
development concept
ERDC

Federal regional planning

- Scope for regional planning policy
orientation and action

State regional planning
in Schleswig-Holstein

- State regional plan
- Regional plans for 5 planning regions

Communal plans

- Regional development
concept

- District development plans

- Master plans of the
communes

*Overview of the
various planning
levels*

Figure 1 Overview of the various planning levels.

detailed regulations. Scope is deliberately left for individual decisions, but these goals are binding for all agencies of public administration. This means that the communes in Germany have the right to regulate their own communal affairs within the framework of the laws.

14

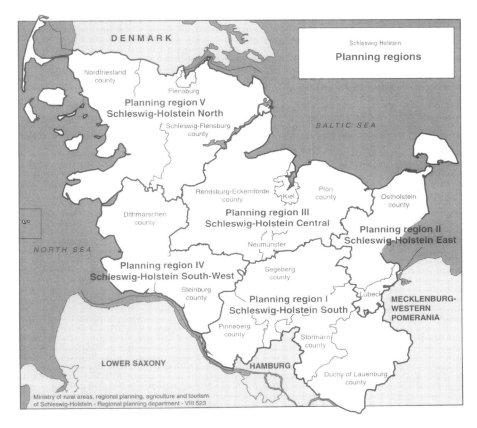

Figure 2 The Planning Regions of Schleswig–Holstein.

When a commune wants to make plans for its area, it draws up a master plan which is also known as an urban land-use plan. The urban land-use plan sets down the location of industrial areas, tenements, streets, recreation areas and open space structures within their territory. When drawing up these plans, the commune has to stay within the goals and aims stated by the Regional Planning Department in their regional plans. The latter will check to see that the commune has done this. The Regional Planning Department, therefore, comments upon every urban land-use plan produced by the communes in Schleswig–Holstein.

As these plans are valid for 15 years, they cannot cover every aspect of spatial planning. Hence there are also regional planning procedures. In these procedures all spatial elements of larger individual projects, such as the construction of energy lines, the extraction of gravel or the location of large-scale retail shops are brought together and they assist in finding the best places for these projects. The over-riding goals of the process are to reveal planning intentions early on to avoid mistakes and to establish whether the project is compatible with regional and state planning goals and, if not, under what circumstances this compatibility can be achieved.

Besides these formal tasks there is also a growing need for informal tasks. For example, the co-operation of communes has a long history in the fields of waste disposal and water supply. Over the last few years, there has been a growing trend for regional initiatives and regional management to supplement regional plans, particularly when implementing state development and regional policy and promoting the development of towns and villages, industry and the infrastructure, as well as nature areas. The communes in Schleswig–Holstein work together in a variety of fields such as tourism and industrial areas. Others are drawing up a concept for their region which deals with a number of fields. In some cases, only two or three communes are involved whereas in others there can be up to 100, and in one case three federal states participated.

The Regional Planning Department plays different roles in these co-operative projects ranging from, accompanying the process as a guest, initiating a project then turning it over to the regional participants, to being an equal partner.

These are the informal tasks which are becoming more and more important for the Regional Planning Department but our main task is still the drawing up of regional plans which includes stating goals, and checking to see that they are being kept by other offices.

3

THE HISTORIC ENVIRONMENT IN THE PRACTICAL WORK OF THE DEPARTMENT OF SPATIAL PLANNING IN SCHLESWIG–HOLSTEIN

Ernst Hansen

I would like to give some examples of practical co-operation between the Department of Spatial Planning and the authorities engaged in preserving the historic environment.

For some time, spatial planning has confined itself to major development predications in 'spatial plans'. These predications include: traffic, housing, industry and settlement axes. Concerns for archaeological and historical sites, however, are brought into all relevant planning processes by the authorities in charge.

Bearing this in mind, there has been a decrease in archaeological and historical aspects in the new generation of spatial plans such as the 1998 state regional plan and the two new regional plans for 'Central' and 'North' Schleswig–Holstein. This concentration on the major tasks of spatial planning does not imply that spatial planning is not concerned with individual cases of preservation of the historic environment, surveys and their evaluation.

I will now give some examples, which distinguish between the levels of spatial planning (see Chapter 2)

SPATIAL PLANS OF SCHLESWIG-HOLSTEIN: DRAWING UP AND CONTENT

The 1998 state regional plan, as a general guideline to regional planning at a federal state level, does not contain any predication concerning historic environments.

The concept of the new regional plan for the planning region of Schleswig–Holstein 'North', however, embodies a multitude of goals pointing out special preservation areas, related to the historic environment.

The preservation areas include the:

- City of Flensburg: historic centre
- City of Husum: preservation of the townscape and the maintenance of historical sites
- City of Tönning: historic remains of the harbour
- City of Wyk auf Föhr: silhouette of the isle, the landscape and the old frieze villages
- City of Friedrichstadt: the historic townscape of the old Dutch settlement
- City of Schleswig: its historic importance and outstanding position on the River Schlei

as well as detailed statements about the importance of these historic sites and their protection.

The following three examples demonstrate the rivalry between the interests of the exploitation of natural resources, of nature preservation, settlements and, last but not least, historic environments, which arose in the process of drawing up the Regional Plan for 'Central' Schleswig–Holstein:

Kosel-Gammelby-Barkelsby, north-west of the city of Eckernförde
According to the surveys of the Federal State Authorities for Nature and Environment, large natural resources exist in this area. In the course of hearing the views of the different parties about the regional plan, increased areas for the exploitation of natural resources were demanded by the organisation in charge of gravel. Finally the Federal State Authorities for Nature and Environment supported the reservation of an additional area for exploitation.

In the following meetings, it became obvious that important archaeological sites were located within this proposed additional area (the 'Osterwall with adjunctive walls' and several grave mounds). The State Authorities for Archaeology pointed out the importance of protecting the land surrounding these historical sites.

As a result, the designation of an additional area for the exploitation of natural resources close to the surface was abandoned because of the importance of these archaeological and historical sites.

This example using the Regional Plan of 'Central' Schleswig–Holstein can be transferred to the recent process of drawing up the Regional Plan for the Planning Region 'North'. The concerns of the State Authorities for Archaeology for grave mounds and their surrounding areas were taken into consideration when areas for exploitation were to be reserved.

Areas for wind turbines

Extraordinary problems occurred in Schleswig–Holstein, when all five regional plans were updated in order to define suitable areas for the siting of wind turbines.

The Federal State Authorities for the Preservation of Historic Sites had sent maps of the counties to the regional planning authorities, on which areas around historic sites which had to be kept clear were marked.

At numerous sites, these spaces modify the borders of the suitable areas for wind turbines.

In the county of Steinburg (near the City of Wilster and the municipality of Neuenbrook), there has been a major reduction in the number of potential sites for wind turbines in order to take care of the land surrounding historic sites.

In the municipality of Schwedeneck, an acceptable compromise has also been reached between the concerns of the State Authorities for Archaeology for grave mounds and the requests for land for wind turbines.

REGIONAL PLANNING PROCEDURES BY SPATIAL PLANNING AUTHORITIES

In contrast to the drawing up of spatial plans, the 'regional planning procedures' allow a preliminary survey of special projects, mostly big infra-structural projects, which have great impact on the development of an area. Generally, all concerned parties (authorities and populace) participate in these procedures. Concerns for historic sites are taken into consideration by participating authorities. These authorities have to bring their requests into the planning procedures in order to oppose the interests of the project supporters.

The objective is to find a compromise in the potential conflict between 'project' and 'historic environment' in the preliminary stages, or to show project supporters that their infra-structural projects cannot be realised because of their interference with historical sites.

Two examples to illustrate these points are as follows:

Exploitation of sand in Fiendskamp in the municipality of Gönnebek

This project favoured the exploitation of sand and gravel. However, in the preliminaries of the 'regional planning procedure' there has been extensive co-ordination with the State Authorities for Archaeology because the suspected 'Battlefield of Bornhöved' may be located within the designated exploitation area. As a result of the co-ordination between all participating parties (including the authorities for the preservation of the historic environment), the right to exploit sand and gravel was granted in such a way that it did not interfere with the historic sites.

Erection of an antenna mast in the Community of Gettorf
The former German Telecom (Deutsche Bundespost) applied for permission to erect an 118 ft high antenna mast close to the medieval church (almost 205 ft high) in the Community of Gettorf. The Federal State Authorities for the Preservation of Historic Sites objected strongly to this proposal as the antenna mast would be in conflict with the church tower. On visiting the location, it became obvious that the mast would severely damage the outlook of the church which is a protected monument. The authorities in charge, therefore, made strong objections to the building of the mast, and as a result, German Telecom decided not to erect it.

REALISATION OF EXISTING GOALS OF REGIONAL PLANNING IN URBAN LAND USE PLANS

Conflict arises on different levels of this process with regard to the development of settlement areas and the protection of the historic environment. Spatial planning authorities participate in the process of drawing up a 'preparatory land-use plan' and 'binding land-use plans', in order to ensure that they comply with the guidelines laid down in their spatial plans. The authorities for the preservation of historic sites also participate in and carry their requests into the preparation of the land-use plan. I would like to demonstrate this part of our work by giving three examples:

Municipality of Maasbüll
The municipality of Maasbüll is situated in the eastern hilly landscape in north-east Schleswig–Holstein. The community has historic sites in two villages and several archaeological sites in the surrounding countryside. There is an area of grave mounds to the south-east of the village. There is also the church in Rüllschau which, together with its graveyard, is an extremely important historic site.

It was very important to take the historic sites into consideration when designating new housing areas in the 'preparatory land-use plan'. This was achieved by placement of the designated housing areas. The archaeological sites were marked in the 'preparatory land-use plan' to show their special need for protection.

Isle of Sylt – Tinnum-Burg
On the Isle of Sylt, the Tinnum-Burg is an important archaeological site. For 25 years now the Federal State Authorities for the Preservation of Historic Sites have been watching the surrounding area closely. In recent urban land-use planning in the City of Westerland an agreed distance from this protected earthen wall was achieved with the support of the Department of Spatial Planning.

City of Schleswig – the old brickyard
I would like to close my discussion with an example in which the Department of Spatial Planning – as an exception – did not follow the reasoning of the Federal State Authorities for Archaeology.

The Department of Spatial Planning had to balance arguments concerning the 'remains' of a terminal part of the 'Danewerk', the historic border wall in the City of Schleswig, which is a significant archaeological site and is protected. According to a request from the city, the site of an old brickyard, which lay close to the 'Danewerk', was supposed to be designated as a building area. It is important to know that the surrounding area of this historic environment was already severely burdened with motorways, railways and roads. Additionally, this part of the 'Danewerk' was covered by debris, and externally was recognisable only as agricultural land.

The archaeological authorities tried to prevent the designation of the property as a building area although the brickyard already existed.

As far as the Department of Spatial Planning was concerned other interests had to be taken into consideration, apart from the historic environment. This resulted in the following answer to the Archaeological State Authorities:

> The intended total denial cannot be granted because of superior aspects of spatial planning. The lack of settlement areas in the City of Schleswig which as a city centre is part of a major development plan prohibits this denial.

CONCLUSION

These examples show the enormous significance of the historic environment in the work of the Department of Spatial Planning in Schleswig–Holstein and, therefore, demonstrate the support of the authorities for the preservation of the historic environment. Nevertheless, the Department of Spatial Planning has to balance the interests of these authorities and those of other parties. Each individual case undergoes a thorough survey and estimation. As a result, Spatial Planners have to decide whether the 'historic environment' succeeds in being protected totally or only partially.

4

THE DANISH NATIONAL APPROACH TO SPATIAL PLANNING AND THE CULTURAL ENVIRONMENT

Carsten Paludan-Müller

What is called the heritage in Britain is known in Denmark by the more technocratic term of the cultural environment. This choice of words could be taken as an illustration of the attempt to underline the importance of an integrated approach to the historic elements in our surroundings. Ironically however we do consider the British heritage administration to be the most advanced in a 'holistic' approach.

It is only as recently as 1994 that Denmark initiated the full incorporation of the landscape dimension into the approach to heritage management, with a newspaper article by the Minister of the Environment announcing the cultural environment as the third dimension of environmental policy.

The responsibility for the management and protection of the cultural environment is shared between several ministries, the County Councils, and the municipalities.

On the national level the Ministry of Culture and the Ministry of Environment and Energy are the key organisations. Other ministries involved in particular issues are the Ministry of Churches (responsible for church buildings), the Ministry of Defence (responsible for historic military buildings and fortifications), and the Ministry of Towns and Housing (responsible for various other historic buildings such as castles owned by the state).

The Ministry of Culture (the State Antiquarian with the local museums as sub-contractors) is the national authority responsible for archaeological rescue excavations and for the documentation of non-scheduled cultural environments under change. In spring 2001, new museum legislation was passed by parliament which provides the basis for a new administrative framework.

The Ministry of Environment and Energy is the national planning authority issuing rules and guidelines for planning on the regional (county) and the local (municipal) level. Through the National Forest and Nature Agency, the Ministry has the national authority for scheduled historic buildings and monuments. This encompasses the authority to include such objects in the list and to grant dispensation partly or entirely from the protection provided by the list. Furthermore the Agency is the national authority on scheduling, in particular landscapes, for protection on the basis of criteria which may include or even entirely relate to cultural environmental qualities.

The Agency also initiates restoration projects on both individual monuments (for example, dolmens and castle ruins) and landscapes. Currently, one of the most important developments is the growing attempt to integrate biological and cultural environmental aspects in the restoration of landscapes.

The counties are responsible for monitoring the physical integrity of the scheduled monuments and also for the administration of the eventual dispensation from the 100 m protective zone around them.

The municipalities are responsible for the eventual inclusion and exclusion of buildings into a municipal list of buildings worthy of preservation. This classification offers much weaker protection than the national scheduling of a building as protected. However, it does oblige the municipal authorities to make a public announcement if permission is given to demolish a building which is included on the list as worthy of preservation.

Furthermore, the counties as regional planning authorities, in compliance with new guidelines issued by the Ministry of Environment and Energy, are now in the process of defining areas of particular value as cultural environments in the planning for the open landscape for the period 2001–2005. This is a novelty, which is particularly important since it establishes the historic environment as an equal issue in the planning process. However it is important to emphasise that the Ministry's instructions are not specific regarding the qualitative and quantitative details of how the areas of cultural environmental value should be selected. To help the process in a suggestive way, the Ministry has published a series of reports on pilot projects which were conducted in two regions. The final and concluding report *CHIP (Cultural Heritage in Planning)* is available in an English edition.[1] The reports offer a method and a variety of examples for the identification of valuable areas, and relevant protective measures and guidelines for their protection, management and administration. The extent to which these reports have actually been used by the counties varies greatly.

In fact we are now at the very important stage of harvesting experience from the results of the different approaches of the counties to the selection of areas of cultural environmental value. The results will be used in the further development of methods, recommendations, and ministerial guidelines for the next planning period. The way that the Ministry of Environment and Energy can assist with this development is through continued dialogue with the counties and through initiatives such as the scheduling of monuments and the restoration of monuments and historic landscapes in those areas selected by the counties for their cultural environment qualities.

It is important, however, to accept that the success and dynamics of the continued development of the cultural environment as an integrated aspect of public planning relies heavily on regional commitment and variation in approach.

In order to promote public debate on cultural environmental issues in a regional and local context, a law was passed by the Minister of Environment and Energy in 1988 to support the formation of a Council of Cultural Environment in each county. The Councils have no official authority to alter the decisions made by the planning authorities. However, when the Building Protection Act was revised this spring, Councils were given the authority to include a building on the local list of those worthy of preservation. This may not save a building from eventual demolition as the municipality still holds the authority to exclude the building from the list. It does, however, force an explicit political decision process on the matter.

The Councils were mainly set up to discuss the decisions affecting the cultural environment, and to offer advice that might stimulate public debate and the foundations of the political and administrative decision process. The greatest hope for the positive development of the cultural environment lies with the continued growth of public awareness of and engagement in a sustainable management of the historic qualities of our landscapes.

References

1.   Danish Forest and Nature Agency, *CHIP (Cultural Heritage in Planning)*, 2001.

5

THE LANDSCAPE AND CULTURAL HERITAGE OF THE WADDEN SEA REGION (LANCEWAD)

Dré van Marrewijk

INTRODUCTION

Off the west coast of Denmark and Schleswig–Holstein and the north coast of Lower Saxony and the Netherlands lies an arc-shaped chain of low-lying islands: the Friesian Islands. These islands are separated from the mainland by a narrow lagoon, varying in width from five to 32 kms. This shallow lagoon with tidal flats, intersected by tidal channels, is called the Wadden Sea. The Wadden Sea makes up only a small part of the North Sea, but it is still the largest wetland area in Europe. The Wadden Sea is an area of outstanding natural beauty, and its tidal flats form the largest unbroken stretch of marine mudflats in the world. It is characterised by high biological diversity and high natural dynamics. Thousands of birds that live in Arctic regions in summer, come to this area to winter. This common store of natural beauty, and the increasing cross-border threats to its environment posed by pollution and general mistreatment, has inspired the Governments of Denmark, the Netherlands and the Federal Republic of Germany to co-operate in the protection and management of the Wadden Sea since 1978.

THE TRILATERAL WADDEN SEA CO-OPERATION

In 1997 the ministers responsible for the protection of the Wadden Sea met in the German town of Stade. They agreed to adopt the Wadden Sea Plan. In the Stade Declaration, the ministers recognised that the Wadden Sea Area is

The Captain's house.   ©*Adriaan Haartsen and Dré van Marrewijk*

28

more than a trilateral nature reserve. It was not only wind, mud and water that created the region. This flat, open and windy stretch of land between Esbjerg in Denmark and Den Helder in the Netherlands has been inhabited for at least two and a half thousand years, in some places even much longer. The topography of the contemporary landscape is, to a large degree, determined by the way it was used and shaped by man through time. There is an intimate relationship between the landscape and the economic and social development in the coastal area. The Wadden Sea Plan even goes so far as to state that the cultural-historic and landscape values are equivalent to the area's natural values. And they are an important basis for the future development of the area. It was therefore agreed to pay attention to this aspect as the third dimension of the trilateral Wadden Sea Co-operation, in addition to ecology and environment.

The countries defined the following four targets for this common heritage:

1.   to preserve, restore and develop the elements that contribute to the character, or identity, of the landscape;
2.   to maintain the full variety of cultural landscapes typical to the Wadden Sea region;
3.   to conserve the cultural heritage; and
4.   to pay special attention to the environmental perspective of the cultural landscape in the context of management and planning.

Protection by national legislation and proper planning should enable integrated maintenance and development of the landscape. At the same time, awareness of the unique cultural-historic and landscape values should be enhanced, because it is important for the understanding of, and the identification with, the landscape and cultural heritage. Finally, the three countries will aim for the Wadden Sea Area, or parts of it, to be nominated as a World Heritage site because of its unique natural and cultural-historic values.

To meet these targets, the governments agreed upon the trilateral LANCEWAD project: an inventory and mapping of the most important landscape and cultural-historic elements of the Wadden Sea Area. It was even agreed that this project should not only map the trilateral co-operation area, consisting of the actual Wadden Sea and the islands, but that the area of investigation should be extended to relevant adjacent areas on the mainland *i.e.* to the Wadden Sea Region as a whole. Furthermore, it was agreed that the project should include an assessment of which elements should be maintained and developed, and recommendations for their protection and utilisation.

From the end of 1999, project teams in Denmark, Schleswig–Holstein, Lower Saxony and the Netherlands started the project, co-ordinated by the Common Wadden Sea Secretariat in Wilhelmshaven, Germany. The results of the investigation will be presented at the ninth Trilateral Governmental Conference in Esbjerg in October 2001.

THE MAKING OF THE CULTURAL LANDSCAPE OF THE WADDEN SEA REGION

What makes the cultural landscape of the Wadden Sea Region so special, so unique? Firstly, there is the geographical aspect. The area forms part of a line of sand dunes that stretches along the European coastline from Skagen in the north of Denmark to Dunkerque in the north of France. In the Wadden Sea area this sandy coastal barrier has been breached by the estuaries of some of north-west Europe's major rivers: the Elbe, Weser, Ems and even a tributary of the Rhine, as well as some minor rivers and creeks. At other places, the dune coast has been breached by storm tides. North of Hamburg, the coastal barrier has been swept away completely. This action of the sea means that the Wadden Sea coastline has been split up into small islands and sand banks, with tidal inlets in between. The sea enters through these inlets at each high tide and floods the lagoon behind. As the tide ebbs, the sandy banks fall dry. This situation has existed since about 2000 BC. At that time there were mudflats, salt marshes, swamps and bogs in the lagoon behind the sand barrier. When more and more breaches in the barrier occurred, the daily tides and changing currents were easily able to erode the peat of the bogs and moors. We can still see this at the Schwimmende Moor ('Floating Moor'), in the Jade Basin of Lower Saxony.

OCCUPATION OF THE SALT MARSHES

During the Iron Age, the area of salt marsh expanded. Each new flood deposited sand and clay on the banks, which silted up higher and higher, until they were only flooded at high tides. Eventually it became possible to live there. The first settlers of the salt marshes appeared some 2,500 years ago in the north of the Netherlands and Lower Saxony. Most probably, the first inhabitants lived in flat settlements. But, as the flood-waters regularly invaded the marsh land, the inhabitants were forced to build their homesteads on artificial dwelling mounds, made up of clay, dung and the accumulation of debris produced by habitation. This is what Pliny the Elder must have seen in the first century AD, when he wrote his famous words about the inhabitants of Frisia, 'resembling sailors in ships when the water covers the surrounding land, but shipwrecked people when the tide has retired'.

Despite the fact that the inhabitants were only protected from high floods by their mounds, the region flourished from the eighth century onwards.

Hogebeintum.   *©Adriaan Haartsen and Dré van Marrewijk*

Oldseadyke.   *©Adriaan Haartsen and Dré van Marrewijk*

31

The soil was extremely fertile and agricultural production was so high, that trade in agricultural goods such as grain, oxen and leather became important. Transport was, of course, by water. As agricultural production grew, so did the population. Thousands of dwelling mounds were erected and hamlets grew into villages. A characteristic pattern of radial or irregular plots developed around these agrarian villages.

In these early medieval times Christianity was brought to the region by missionaries like St. Boniface[1], the Apostle of Germany, who was killed by a Frisian mob in Dokkum in 754, and St. Ansgar, the Apostle of Scandinavia. The first churches were most probably built of wood and no longer exist, but many of the Romanesque churches that were built some centuries later have survived. Most of them are built of the red brick that still characterises the region.

Some of the dwelling mounds prospered from trade and grew together into ribbon-like mounds, like the trading towns Langwarden, Groothusen, Emden and Leeuwarden. Others have remained tiny villages to this day or can be found as abandoned farm mounds dotted throughout the marshland.

EMBANKING OF THE MARSHES

The first dykes were built in Roman times. These dykes only protected small stretches of arable land in summer-time. Around AD 1000 people started to construct dykes to enclose the low-lying marsh lands. These dykes acted as a barrier against winter floods. First a dyke was constructed around stretches of land belonging to one or more villages. Later these so-called island-polders were connected by arm-dykes, that dammed off intermediate streams and creeks. These dykes still had a merely defensive character. Monasteries played a major role in the occupation and the construction of dykes along the northern coast of the Netherlands and on the islands.

The main reason for building embankments, and to create vast areas of freshwater marsh land, was to exploit new arable land and pasture. A system had to be developed to dispose of the rainfall and river water from the hinterland. A network of canals and dykes criss-crosses the flat polder land to provide an artificial drainage system, keeping the land dry. The water was drained out to sea through sluices, which meant that locks had to be constructed for transport to and from the sea.

Land reclamation even became a Dutch export product. In the twelfth century the Archbishop of Bremen drew settlers from the Netherlands to the Elbe-region in order to close off the low-lying areas of the Elbe marshes with dykes and drainage systems, and to cultivate the land. These methods were later copied by the local inhabitants.

Staede. ©*Adriaan Haartsen and Dré van Marrewijk*

Mongeltonder. ©*Adriaan Haartsen and Dré van Marrewijk*

A new phase of reclamation started just before 1500. In fact at this point in history, the famous 'struggle against the sea' really started. From this time, extensive land reclamation programmes took place to increase potential farming areas. In the Netherlands, the Frisian Wadden region was brought under centralised government. This, together with rising prices for agricultural products, urbanisation and the availability of capital from the towns in Holland, led to a boom in dyke-building. The Bildt polders in Friesland and the Wieringerwaard and Zijpe-polder in North-Holland were laid out geometrically, following the Renaissance revival of classical principles of land parcellation. From the sixteenth century onwards, windmills came into use to pump the excess water from the polders to the sea.

DYKE BREACHES AND FLOODS

Storm tides occurred during the whole period. Sometimes the effects were minor, and today only a sudden bend in the dyke, around a deep scour pond, marks the place where once the dyke was breached. More severe floods caused the loss of land and villages. Between 1250 and 1600, at least 20 disastrous floods were recorded. Regularly storm tides flooded or swept away parts of the area. The cultivated coastal moors were particularly vulnerable, as the draining of these lands led to subsidence of the peat. One storm surge could be enough to swallow vast areas of land, as the examples of the Dollard basin and the disappeared former island of Nordstrand show. Remnants of lost villages and traces of cultivation can still be found on the tidal flats.

The small, unembanked marsh islands in North Friesland, the *halligen*, give a good impression of what the landscape must have looked like after a storm surge. Much of the present mainland in Schleswig–Holstein once consisted of numerous *halligen*, interrupted by tidal inlets. Many of these drowned lands in Schleswig–Holstein were later reclaimed; the former Middelzee in Dutch Friesland was also reclaimed in the late Middle Ages. At other places, major breaches are still recognisable: Zuyderzee (IJsselmeer), Dollard, and the Jade-basin.

The reasons why these disasters occurred are numerous: the rising sea level, changes in currents, a change in weather conditions that caused an increase in storm surges and, probably most importantly, human activity itself. Many breaches of the dykes were caused, or helped, by drainage which lowered the level of the marsh and moor lands. Peat-digging (for fuel or salt extraction) and clay-digging (for dyke building or brick making) also weakened the dykes. Breaches were also caused by poor maintenance of the dyke itself. The famous German novelist Theodor Storm (what's in a name!) – who was born in Husum and wrote about life in this region – tells us about the way the steep and therefore fragile dykes were constructed, and how an enlightened dyke-master tries to convince his fellow peasants to make the dykes stronger. In vain, of course.[2]

FISHING, WHALING AND SHIPPING ON THE WADDEN SEA ISLANDS

Most of the sandy islands in the Wadden Sea are made up of dune ridges, salt marsh and polders. Some have a core of Pleistocene boulder clay, such as Sylt and Amrum in Germany and Texel and Wieringen in the Netherlands. The oldest traces of settlement, dating from the Stone Age and Bronze Age, can be found on these islands.

The islands have continually been subjected to erosion and accretion. Between the seventeenth and twentieth centuries, the East Frisian island of Wangerooge shifted eastwards over half its length. A tower that in 1793 stood in the middle of the island, was at its western edge by 1914. Elsewhere villages like Sier on Ameland disappeared into the sea. But on the other hand, islands grew together (as was the case with Texel and Eierland) or an island grew together with the mainland (Callantsoog and Huisduinen in north Holland, Skallingen in Denmark). This process was helped along by the construction of a man-made sand dyke.

Apart from some arable and livestock farming, hunting, fishing and shipping have long been the main sources of income on the islands. Some villages on the islands eventually concentrated fully on fishing and shipping. The thatched fishermens' houses in Nordby and Sønderho (on the Danish island of Fanø) are now a tourist attraction. Tourism has long since been another source of income on the islands. The German island of Norderney has been a bathing resort since 1797, the oldest in Germany and the Wadden Sea region as a whole.

TRADE

Harbours were developed along the coast to facilitate fishing and trade. Trade in amber has been important since prehistoric times. In the days of the Vikings the Danish town of Ribe became a centre of trade between Scandinavia, England and north-west Europe. It became the home of skilled craftsmen who worked and traded in amber, glass and leather. Ribe reached its height in the twelfth century. The basis of trade was the export of agricultural products to Flanders and the buying and selling of textiles and luxury goods from the south. The influence of the Vikings has been felt throughout the whole region, and far beyond. In 1996 a Viking treasure was found on the former island of Wieringen in north Holland, which included silver coins from Arabia. It symbolises the extent of their influence.

Other towns developed during the High Middle Ages on favourable sites on the higher rim of sandy soil, especially where there were navigable water courses. Towns like Hjerting and Tønder, Husum and Hamburg, Stade and Bremen, Oldenburg, and Groningen became important as harbours, trading posts and regional administrative centres.

Between 1250 and 1350 the Hanseatic League was formed. This association of medieval north German cities later expanded to Sweden, Holland and Flanders. The League was at its height from 1350–1500. Many towns in the Wadden Sea profited from their membership of the League.

Apart from the fishing of herring, cod and sole, from the sixteenth century whaling became a lucrative means of support. Whaling was at first concentrated in the Netherlands, especially on the Wadden Sea islands of Terschelling and Ameland, but the industry attracted seafarers from the whole region. The interiors of homes and farms on the Danish island of Rømø are richly decorated with tableaux of Dutch tiles, illustrating the prosperity that shipping brought the islanders in those days.

In the seventeenth century, the Dutch economy flourished thanks to the trade with the East and West Indies. The ports of Amsterdam and other trading towns in the Zuyderzee were only accessible via the Wadden Sea. Due to their strategic location, shipping became more and more important on the islands and the Wadden Sea region supplied hundreds of qualified sea-farers. The island of Fanø for instance possessed a large fleet of sailing ships at the end of the eighteenth and during the whole nineteenth century. After Denmark lost parts of Schleswig–Holstein to Germany, a new fishing and shipping harbour was built in 1868 at Esbjerg.

At the end of the eighteenth century the Dutch government based its navy in Den Helder. Strong fortifications were built around the naval base in the Napoleonic period. A century later, Wilhelmshaven was erected as a naval base in Germany.

RECENT CHANGES OF THE CULTURAL LANDSCAPE

Life of course did not stop in the nineteenth century, neither did the changing of the landscape. In fact, most of the landscape changes and most of the buildings and infrastructure date from the last two centuries. Let me just give an incomplete shortlist of more or less recent elements, that all illustrate a specific phase in recent history and that now are part of the Wadden Sea landscape:

• farmsteads, barns and duck decoys

- windmills and pumping stations
- roads, canals and railways
- industrial mills and factories
- schools, court houses and town halls
- lighthouses, beacons and ship wharfs
- inns and tourist hotels
- fortifications and the Atlantic Wall
- sporting grounds and ice rinks
- and finally … new reclamations and dykes again.

The final stage of reclamation in the Netherlands started in the 1920s under the direction of the civil engineer and minister of Public Works, Cornelius Lely. The Afsluitdijk, the large dam between Friesland and north Holland, closed the Zuyderzee off from the Wadden Sea. The building of the dam enabled the reclamation of almost 2000 sq kms (800 sq miles) of land in the former Zuyderzee, creating four new polders. Finally, in 1969 the Lauwers basin was embanked.

THE LANCEWAD PROJECT

What has all this to do with the LANCEWAD project? In this project, we are mapping all of the cultural landscape elements that are of importance in understanding the region's history. Project teams in each district make their own database, based on information from existing electronic data, literature, fieldwork, experts and local people. Thirty-three elements or groups of elements are distinguished. Each element is divided into different types (Table 1). For example: the element 'dwelling mound' can be a 'village or town mound', a 'church mound' or a 'farm mound'. Each object that we map has to fit into one of these categories.

For each object, extra information is added regarding the name, topography, the date of origin, condition, historical value, protection status, together with an overall assessment (Table 2). This enormous database will be transferred to a GIS-environment, so that new information can be obtained. For example, geographical dispersal of different elements, the characteristics that make up the common identity of the whole area and regional differences, etc.

THREATS

As I have said, the landscape of the Wadden Sea Region has always been in a state of change. This will no doubt continue. But now there is one big difference: changes are taking place more rapidly and on a much larger scale. Agricultural practices, urbanisation, industrialisation, the development of infrastructure, nature development and the growth of tourism all have their effect on the landscape and in turn can pose a threat to the cultural heritage of the Wadden Sea.

The conservation of dykes, for instance, is poor. Usually the first dyke behind the actual sea dyke still serves as a protection if the sea dyke breaks. But all the older dykes lying further inland no longer have a defensive function. If they are used as roads, they usually remain untouched. But old dykes in the middle of farmland are easily shovelled away, as has occurred in the Dutch Dollardpolders. Dwelling mounds are also threatened, especially by housing development and the lowering of the water table.

These two examples show that the identification with the past is disappearing; the landscape is threatened by a 'loss of memory'. The question arises what we can do about it. Our recommendations will be presented to the Governmental Conference in Esbjerg, later this year.

RECOMMENDATIONS

What will these recommendations contain? First of all we are working to identify the characteristics of the region. These elements should be preserved and maintained within their physical and historical context. Legal protection is an option, but not in the first instance. A combination of good physical planning and regional development through integrated planning and management will be recommended. Raising awareness of the values of the cultural heritage and demonstrating how these characteristics can be used to increase the quality of the environment is more likely to gain the support of local governments and local communities. The preservation of the cultural landscape will also be more successful if the relevant stakeholders are involved in the planning and management of the heritage. It has for instance great potential for cultural-historic tourism, now barely exploited. Only by involving the tourism sector can projects to preserve this heritage succeed.

Moreover, the structure of land parcellation and the architectural style of the farmsteads could be a source of inspiration in town development for the creation of new living environments, which reflect the region's identity.

Other recommendations will be made on ways of applying existing national instruments to safeguard the cultural heritage, on monitoring its status and on follow-up projects regarding implementation.

Finally there will be a recommendation concerning the nomination of the region as a cultural World Heritage Site. At the moment, it looks as if the 'exceptional universal value' and a guaranteed and sustainable management of the region will meet the requirements for nomination. A point of more concern is achieving local support for such a nomination. We first have to work on this. We have to convince the inhabitants that a nomination must be seen as a reward for what has been achieved, rather than a means of imposing more severe restrictions and obligations. If we succeed in this, a nomination for the Wadden Sea Region, or at least parts of it, as a cultural World Heritage Site can be achieved within three to four years.

CONCLUSIONS

The Wadden Sea Region is more than Europe's largest wetland and an important nature reserve worth protecting. The region is also a unique cultural landscape. This flat, clay strip of land, divided from the North Sea by a series of sandy barrier islands, has a common history which has led to a rather singular and interesting landscape, that is – by international standards – unique and unrivalled. All over the region the tension can be felt between man's efforts to protect 'hearth and home' on the one hand, and the eternal threat and attraction of the sea on the other hand.

This does not mean that each part of the area is equal: each region has had its own political, social and economic history that is visible in the landscape. A landscape that reflects identity, and that combines unity with diversity. A landscape whose qualities deserve the political attention of the three countries to whom it belongs.

Farmstead.   ©*Adriaan Haartsen and Dré van Marrewijk*

ACKNOWLEDGEMENTS

This paper has been prepared in co-operation with the members of the international project team: Manfred Vollmer (CWSS), Mette Guldberg (Denmark), Gregor Schlicksbier (Lower Saxony), and Matthias Maluck (Schleswig–Holstein).

References

1.   St Boniface, originally named Wynfrith (c. 673–754), was an English monk and missionary, who became known as the Apostle of Germany. In 722 he was appointed bishop by Pope Gregory II, with the responsibility for preaching the gospel throughout Germany. About 745 his own diocese was finally fixed at Mainz but he resigned seven years later, to return to missionary work. On the fifth of June 754 he was killed by a Frisian mob near Dokkum, which still hosts a holy well and is a place of pilgrimage.
2.   Although a new dyke was built by Hauke Haien, the main character of the novel, an older stretch of the dyke broke during a storm surge on All Saints' Eve, due to poor maintenance.

Further Reading

CWSS, *Stade Declaration/Trilateral Wadden Sea Plan 1997*, 1998.
Schroor, M., 'Diking and settlement in the Netherlands up till the building of the Afsluitdijk. The new cultural landscape in the Wadden Sea Region after the Second World War', in *Workshop on the Cultural Heritage in the Wadden Sea Region. Ribe, September 10th–12th 1997. Abstracts and Lectures,* The National Forest and Nature Agency, 1997.
Storm, T., *Der Schimmelreiter, 1988, (The Dykemaster,* English translation by Denis Jackson, 1996).
Waterbolk, H.T., 'The cultural heritage of the Wadden landscape', in *Workshop on the Cultural Heritage in the Wadden Sea Region. Ribe, September 10th–12th 1997. Abstracts and Lectures,* The National Forest and Nature Agency, 1997.
Waterbolk, H.T., *Basisdocument deel 2: landschappelijke verscheidenheid (onvolledig concept),* 1999.

Table 1 Lancewad inventory elements and types.

no	element	type
01	dwelling mound	village/town mound – church mound - farm mound – dyke mound; round – elongated/rectangular; not built on
02	village	concentric/round – elongated/linear; mound-, dyke-, sluice (Siel)-, canal-, harbor-, road (Hufen) village
03	agrarian building	farm – adjoining building (barn/shed/haystack/granary); Uthländisches Haus – Geesthardenhaus – Barghus – Gulfhaus - Hallenhaus - Kop(hals)romp - Ostfiesian/Oldambtster – Haubarg/Bargscheune/stelp
04	charact. field pattern	radial – parallel - block; regular – irregular; ditches – trees – earthen walls; vaulted arable land
21	dyke	actual sea dyke - old dyke – summer dyke – sand dyke – dam – embankment/Sietwende
22	ditch/waterway	natural watercourse - dug watercourse/drainage canal - moat/ditch
23	sluice	lock/weir – sluice (Siel)
24	land reclamation	
25	pumping station/polder mill	pumping station – polder mill; tjasker – Dutch windmill – American windmill
26	freshwater supply	pool (Fething) – ring dyke pool – water tower – well - Scheetel (rain water collection system)
27	wheel/breach pond	
41	city	town rights
42	maritime settlement	
43	fishery and hunting	fishery – hunting; duck decoy; camp site
44	harbor	harbor (in use) – old harbor – embarkation place – anchorage
45	craft or industry	craft; ship wharf – industrial factory – milk/fodder factory – fish factory – mineral assimilation
46	navigation	lighthouse – rescue station – seamark
47	bridge, ferry, ford	fixed bridge – movable bridge – ferry – ford
49	mining	clay-, sand-, peat-, salt-, shells/chalk-, gas/oil mining
50	canal (*transport*)	canal

Table 1 Lancewad inventory elements and types continued.

51	road, path, rail	road – path – railway ; towing path – church path – ring road – ravine (Hohlweg) – military road (Heerweg) – dyke passage
52	shipwreck	on land – in sea
53	place of trade and travel	market place– inn – station – store house
54	(industrial) mill	windmill – watermill ; sawing mill – graining mill – oil mill – paper mill
71	castle/manor/estate	castle – stronghold – manor/estate ; garden/park
72	church	church – chapel – synagogue ; belfry – bell cage
73	monastery	
74	burial place	church yard – Jewish graveyard – burial field – burial mound – chambered tomb
75	other building	urban ensemble - dwelling house – town hall – court house – water board building – dyke storehouse – school
76	historical place	historical place – pilgrimage – memorial stone/statue
77	military object	naval harbor – bunker/casemate – defense line – fort/sconce – fortification (city)
86	tourism/recreational facility	hotel - skating ground – fivel ground – skating tour – walking tour
95	other	historical boundary

42

Table 2 Attributes of the LANCEWAD database.

Field
object_id
country_id
region_id
element_id
object_no
name
place
parish
date
period
condition
vulnerability
hist_value
protection_id
overall_assessment
accessibility
context
remarks

6

THE ROOTS OF THE CULTURAL HERITAGE IN THE COASTAL AREA
Landscape Development and Settlement History in the Salt Marshes of Schleswig–Holstein

Dirk Meier

The cultural landscapes in Europe reflect its rich cultural heritage in their diversity. Cultural landscapes are the result of human impact upon the environment, and are the archives of our history. The importance of the cultural landscape has been stated in the perspectives for European Spatial Development which resulted from a meeting of European Union (EU) spatial planning ministers in Glasgow in 1998. There is virtually no landscape in Europe which can be classed primarily as natural landscape. Cultural landscapes are found in the most remote and extreme parts of Europe ranging from coastal (including the landscape of the North Sea) to high alpine areas. The new cultural landscape project – founded by the Culture 2000 programme of the EU and including different projects in several European countries – will demonstrate this. The lead partner in this project is the community of Albersdorf in Dithmarschen, together with the Department of Coastal Archaeology of the Research and Technology Centre, University of Kiel.

The cultural heritage of the Wadden Sea and the coastal area of north-western Europe is closely linked with landscape development. The Wadden Sea area is a region of great natural and cultural importance. Since 1978 the governments of Denmark, the Netherlands and the Federal Republic of Germany have jointly co-operated in the trilateral Wadden Sea plans for the protection and management of the Wadden Sea. In the 8th Trilateral Wadden Sea Plan, the environmental ministries of Germany, Denmark and the Netherlands declared their international interest in the cultural heritage of the Wadden Sea Area as a whole.[1] The status of the landscape today is determined by the way it was shaped by man. The dykes, ditches and the cultivated landscape still follow the natural creek and lagoon system of the salt marshes. In 1997, the ministers declared that:

> The cultural-historic and landscape values of the area are closely linked to the economic and social development of the coastal area and, by international standards, are unique and unrivalled. The cultural-historic and landscape values are equivalent to the area's natural values and are an important basis for the development of tourism. The cultural-historic and landscape heritage and the diversity between the regions are essential for understanding the development and identity of the area and the inhabitants' identification with the landscape. It was agreed at the Leeuwarden (the Netherlands) Conference in 1994 that, in addition to the natural and environmental dimensions, attention should be paid to this aspect as the third dimension in the trilateral Wadden Sea co-operation.

In 1998, an international steering commitee (WADCULT) was set up to manage the trilateral policy, and was followed by a working group on the Landscape and Cultural Heritage of the Wadden Sea (LANCEWAD) in 2000. The LANCEWAD project, which is partly funded by the Interreg North Sea Programme of the EU from 2000–2001, includes an inventory and a GIS map of the landscape and cultural heritage of the Wadden Sea, an assessment of which elements should be maintained and developed, and recommendations for their protection.The most important elements of the cultural heritage in the Wadden Sea are the *Wurten*, the dykes and the field forms and how they are linked together. The settlement pattern and field form structure are therefore very important for understanding the landscape. In Schleswig–Holstein this project is co-ordinated by the Department of Coastal Archaeology of the Research and Technology Centre of the University of Kiel, under my project leadership. Our work is closely linked with that of the State Archaeology Service of Schleswig–Holstein.

The LANCEWAD project is the subject of another paper in this volume written by Dré van Marrewijk, a member of the project team. I will, therefore, discuss the roots of cultural heritage in the Wadden Sea area: the landscape and settlement history. As there is not enough time to talk about the salt marshes from the Ijzzelmeer to Denmark as a whole, I will give some examples from our research in the salt marshes of Schleswig–Holstein.

THE LANDSCAPE

The transformation of the coastal landscape, economy and settlement from the first habitation of the marshes 2000 years ago until the present day is a fascinating topic. The many questions surrounding this subject, such as coastal changes, man and the environment, economics and mobility, and stability of settlements, can only be pointed out through interdisciplinary research. The outstanding importance of wetlands in the North Sea area of Schleswig–Holstein, their environment, their landscape history and their contribution to the past has been well established over the last 50 years.[2,3,4,5,6]

In contrast to other landscapes, the development of the environment and the history of settlement and economy in the wetlands were dominated for a long time by nature, by the changing impact of the sea. The landscape of the North Sea area in Schleswig–Holstein – divided into the areas of Dithmarschen, Eiderstedt and North Frisia – consists predominantly of Quarternary glacial and postglacial deposits (Figure 1).[7] The wetland landscape was significantly changed during the later Holocene as a result of the rising sea-level.

The settlement pattern from the prehistoric period until AD 1000 was totally dependant upon the influence of the sea. The natural environment of the coastal area with its salt marshes, peats and beach ridges formed the history of human habitation. From the prehistoric period onwards, settlements in the salt marshes were mostly erected as ground settlements (*Flachsiedlungen*) or as artificial mounds (*Terpen* or *Wierden* in the Netherlands, *Wurten* or *Warften* in Germany). The presence of prehistoric ground settlements in marshy clay areas indicates that the rise of the Holocene sea level in the past was interrupted by periods of standstill or even of lowering water level.

Land use in the un-dyked marshes reveals a close correlation between relief, settlement and agriculture. Near to the coast, tidal creeks formed a landscape with irregular divisions, which were first inhabited in the Roman and early medieval periods. The tidal creeks and rivers were used as transport routes to the sea and to the hinterland. The salt marshes represent a special settlement area with very specific ecological conditions. Before dyking, which started in the High Middle Ages, salt marshes were much wider than they are today, and because of their good soils they played an important role in agriculture. During the prehistoric period, the grassland areas, necessary for grazing cattle, existed naturally in the salt marshes. Whether arable farming was practised under these extreme ecological conditions has to be proved individually for each settlement. Arable farming was only carried out on a small scale and was restricted to the natural levees of the creeks.

Two ecological factors: frequent inundations and salinity are important, and their combination determines the various possibilities for settlement and economy in the salt marshes. Dwelling mounds (*Wurten, Warften*) and ground-level settlements (*Flachsiedlungen*) often preserved plant remains which means that palaeoecological conditions around them can be reconstructed. The position of the farmed area around the Wurten above Mean High Water (MHW) can thus be determined.[8] The *Wurten* are, therefore, one of the most important elements of the cultural heritage of the Wadden Sea area.

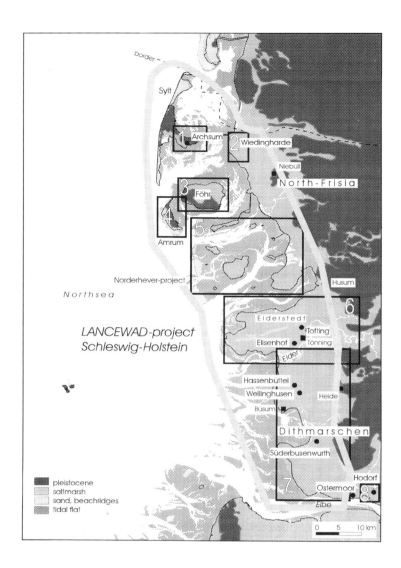

Figure 1 The west coast of Schleswig–Holstein with detailed maps of the Cultural Heritage. 1 Archsum-project; 2 Wiedingharde; 3 Föhr; 4 Amrum; 5 Norderhever-project; 6 Eiderstedt; 7 Dithmarschen; 8 Hodorf. The detailed maps of the coastal archaeology are the basis of the GIS data base of LANCEWAD in Schleswig–Holstein

48

The family of the *Juncetum geradi* was the most important plant around the settlements in the salt marshes. However, the plant varieties that have been recorded in different marsh settlements show that there was considerable variations in their environments.

FROM PREHISTORIC TIMES UNTIL THE LATE PRE-ROMAN PERIOD

Our picture of the prehistoric coastal settlement around the North Sea is incomplete as the encroaching sea has made the reconstruction of settlement history difficult. Ten thousand years ago, the warming of temperatures in the early Holocene, the melting of the ice shield, the following glacio-eustatic sea-level rise and the Holocene transgression of the North Sea influenced the changing configuration of the coastline and the vegetation during the Stone Age. The environment changed from late Palaeolithic to Mesolithic, from tundra to a wooded landscape. Stone artefacts from the bottom of the North Sea are known from these periods, and they indicate that the area was visited by groups of hunter-gatherers. The mapping of the horizontal and vertical distribution of these archaeological finds provides information about the former sea level. The finds of the core and flake-axe culture during the middle Mesolithic (Boreal) in England, the Netherlands and Denmark give the impression that these cultures must have spread over the present southern North Sea, which was still dry in Boreal time. In 6,500 BP, at the peak of the transgression, the North Sea reached the Pleistocene morains of Dithmarschen and North Frisia. In the following period of stagnation or regression, the area of the present North Frisian Wadden Sea was covered with lakes, peats and *phragmites*.

Flint artefacts from the North Frisian Wadden Sea area indicate that these areas were used during the Neolithic period and the Bronze Age.[9] Megalithic graves and flint materials are concentrated on the Pleistocene areas of the North Frisian islands Sylt, Amrum and Föhr (Figure 1). Artefacts from this time, are also known from the beach ridges in Eiderstedt and Dithmarschen.

For 6,500 years, the natural environment of the Dithmarschen coastal area has consisted of a varied woodland landscape on the moraines, combined with lakes and bays, which spread far inland. The different ecological zones (woodland landscape, lakes and bays) provided good resources for hunter-gatherer groups. Sites, like Fedderingen,[10,11] indicate, that the coastal areas were used for fishing, hunting and flint search by the hunter gatherers during the Mesolithic period. A pot of the late Mesolithic Ertebölle-Ellerbek culture was found near Ecklack, which was covered with 3 m of sediment layers. This find indicates that a settlement was possibly flooded over in the late Mesolithic period.

During the Neolithic period, the first beach ridges developed along the coast line in Dithmarschen. The bays were deliminated from the sea, and peat developed in these valleys. The woods, on the Pleistocene moraine landscape, were partly de-forested by the first farmers. Many Neolithic and Bronze Age graves, for example around Albersdorf, are known from these areas.[12] An 'Erdwerk' of the Neolithic culture has been partly excavated near Albersdorf. Many other settlements, known only from flint artefacts rather than houses, are situated between two different ecological areas, the woodland moraine landscape and the peat covered valleys or the woodlands and the sea.

Many urn graves from the pre-Roman period were excavated in Dithmarschen.[13] The fact that the cemeteries are widespread indicates the existence of different nuclear settlement areas, such as those around Meldorf, Burg, Süderhastedt and Meldorf-Hemmingstedt.[14] The edges of the Pleistocene areas, near to the peat-covered valleys and to the silted up salt marshes in the west, were possibly densely populated, but this has not yet been proved by excavation.

THE FIRST STEP INTO THE SALT MARSHES: SETTLEMENTS IN THE ROMAN PERIOD

A major event in settlement history was the habitation of the sea and river marshes, which had gradually silted up and become habitable as the rise in the sea level slowed down. The seaward parts of the wetlands, with a low elevation relative to the sea, are generally within reach of salt water and, therefore, consist of salt marshes and estuaries where marine clays and silts are deposited. In Dithmarschen the seaward silted salt marshes are slightly higher than the landward marshes with their bogs.

The oldest finds from the marsh area of Schleswig–Holstein can be traced back to the early Roman period. Around the time of Christ, a large part of the wetlands had been safe from storm floods for some time. During the period of regression, settlements could be built, for the first time, on the high deposits of the river marsh area of the River Stör and in the sea marsh areas of Dithmarschen, the southern part of Eiderstedt and in the Wiedingharde in North Frisia (Figure 2).

The marsh area of the River Elbe is one of the wetland areas in Schleswig–Holstein which has not yet been surveyed in a new systematic way. The research results in this area are, therefore, more than 60 years old. The Roman settlements in the river marshes adapted themselves strictly to the given natural conditions: the high river banks, tidal channel inversion ridges and the peat zone behind. Archaeological finds, borings and excavations in the Stör marsh in the 1930s have indicated that these high river banks were densely populated in the first and second centuries AD. The peat zone could not be inhabited, and settlements were founded on the uppermost parts of the then still forested elevated levees. The upper parts of the tidal forests were

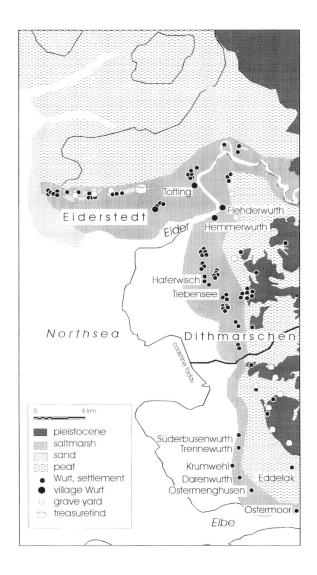

Figure 2 Coastal area of Dithmarschen and Eiderstedt in the Roman period (AD 1–400).

51

destroyed by human activities, and were not able to regain their territory in later occupation phases because the area was used as grazing grounds and fields. A typical example of a river marsh settlement is Hodorf, which was excavated in 1935 by W. Haarnagel (Figure 1).[15] In the excavation, a stable-house from a second century ground settlement was unearthed. From the end of the second century AD until the fourth century AD, a *Wurt* had to be built. It is possible that either the settlements or the marsh area (after habitation) were flooded at the end of the Roman period. Ostermoor is another example of a river marsh settlement. An excavated group of four long stable-houses from the first and second centuries AD was situated in a line near a tidal creek on high clay deposits of the Elbe river marsh.[16] The settlement was abandoned after 150 to 200 years because the extension of the peat in the lowland made agriculture impossible.

Northwards, the marine marshes of Dithmarschen extend from the Elbe in the south to the Eider in the north, lying west of once densely wooded Saale Pleistocene deposits, beach ridges and boggy lowlands. The bay of Meldorf, which has extended far inland in modern times, separated the northern from the southern marsh. New archaeological, geological and palaeobotanical research have led to a good understanding of their evolution. The old marine marsh of Dithmarschen was first occupied with permanent settlements in the first century AD (Figure 2). Previously the marsh areas were possibly used as natural grass-feeding for cattle. The settlements of the Pleistocene sandy soils are not well documented but registration of archaeological finds in similar areas, for example in South-West Jutland, have pointed to a high density of settlements at the edge of the Pleistocene area. Typical settlement pattern on the Pleistocene areas indicates the use of two different ecological ground soils: the wetlands and the wood area with clay and sandy soils. New archaeological, palaeobotanical and geological investigations in the coastal area of Dithmarschen, based on mapping of the cultural heritage, and partly financed by the German Research Council and the local county revealed a good overview of the settlement history of the salt marsh.

In the old marine marsh of southern Dithmarschen, a group of large *Wurten* are stretched out in a long settlement line near to the high medieval dyke. Radiocarbon dates from Darrenwurth and Trennewurth and archaeological finds from Ostermenghusen and Süderbusenwurth indicate that some of these *Wurten* were founded in the Roman period. The inner part of the marsh area was swampy and the older finds of Eddelak have shown that only small settlements existed on inversion-ridges or tidal creek banks. The sea marsh was not populated before the first century. Excavations since 1998 in Süderbusenwurth (Figure 2) indicate the existence of a ground settlement with house-sites on small clay mounds at +1.00 m above Mean Sea Level (MSL). These houses were erected shortly after AD 52 and were surrounded by fences in AD 149/150. Floods caused the settlers to raise the whole settlement with clay and dung. The settlement was abandoned by the end of the third century possibly due to flooding of the low ground of the sea marsh.

In the northern marsh of Dithmarschen, small settlements are streched out in two long lines about 2000 to 4000 m west from the edge of the Pleistocene area of Heide. Archaeological excavations have shown the existence of a ground settlement on the marsh in Tiebensee which is about +1.00 to +1.30 m above MSL (Figure 2). Four to six long houses with wickerwork walls, living quarters and stables for 20 cattle (approx 5 m wide and 20 m long) were built on flat sod mounds. The nearby salt marshes provided a good base for grazing cattle. The settlement was raised a little more in the second and third centuries, and two kilns and a wickerwork well were erected on the old house site. The site was later abandoned by settlers, possibly because of a higher ground water level, which impeded agriculture in the lower marsh near to the Geest. The younger coastal settlements were located westwards, nearer to the coastline.

Various settlements were built near Haferwisch, about 2 km west of Tiebensee, in an area under more marine influence, only +0.5 m above sea level. Investigations in 1992–93 documented the raising of *Wurten* after AD 140. Houses from this site are not known, but different types of wells and water basins have been found. The grave of a dog was excavated at the edge of the settlement. In the third and fourth centuries AD the *Wurt* became larger, before the settlement was abandoned at the end of the fourth century AD (Figure 2).

Another group of Roman period settlements are known from the peninsula of Eiderstedt, north of the River Eider. The formation of the sand ridges was important for the landscape development of the modern peninsula. The deposition of sediments and marshes developed in the middle of the first millenium BC. Marshes mostly emerged to the south of the sand ridges along the River Eider. The areas to the north were protected from direct marine influence by land spits and Pleistocene cores to the north-west, and gradually became boggy.

Habitation of the high marshes along the meandering River Eider did not begin until the first or second centuries AD. The stagnation or regression of the sea and of the storm surge levels on large sections of the North Sea coast permitted the construction of surface-level settlements on the river banks. Because of the renewed rise in sea level, however, the ground settlements soon had to be raised. The Eider estuary has several sites which indicate that this area played a more important role in transport and the economic system. The earliest phase of occupation, from the second century AD onwards, was established along the higher river banks. On the north of the river (the estuary formed in Roman times was a smaller one as today), the *Dorfwurten* of Tofting and possibly Pernör date to the Roman period. These are mirrored on the south bank by the *Dorfwurten,* Hemmerwurth and Flehderwurth, which possibly existed at the same time. The best known excavated example is the

Figure 3 Tofting, Eiderstedt. Dwelling mounds, field pattern and ditches around the Roman period *Wurt* of Tofting.

Dorfwurt of Tofting[17] which was established in a salt meadow on a MSL +1.45 m high river bank , and was populated from the second to the fifth centuries AD (Figure 3). The marsh became increasingly salty during the third and fourth centuries AD.[18] Three house-sites with long, west-east orientated stable-houses were excavated.[19] The wickerwork walls of the houses were protected by clay sod walls. After a house was abandoned, small layers of dung and clay sods were packed up and a new building was erected almost in the same place. House-site I was raised from approximately MSL +1.83 m to MSL +2.45 m in the second century, house-site II from MSL +2.60 m to MSL +2.82 m in the third century and house-site III reached a height of MSL +3.65 m in the fourth century and of MSL +4.08 m in the fifth century.

The high river banks of the Eider protected the marshes behind from floods. These landward, more swampy areas were only settled temporarily. Further settlements existed on the sand ridges, where the dead were buried in urnfields.[20] The early settlers abandoned Eiderstedt during the migration of nations. A hoard containing precious metals which was found buried near Katharinenheerd[21] indicates that these were troubled times.

The marsh areas of Dithmarschen and Eiderstedt were densely populated until the third and fourth centuries.[22,23] Like the settlements, the cremations, which are partly recorded on the beach ridges in Eiderstedt and the Pleistocene areas of Dithmarschen, were abandoned. The last finds from Tofting date to the Migration period, possibly in the fifth or sixth century. The end of habitation in the German North Sea marshes during the migration period may be the result of climate deterioration. On the other hand, however, the political and economic system collapsed during the migration period with the fall of the Roman Empire, and resulted in instability. Little is known about the pattern of habitation between AD 400 to 700 in the marsh area of Schleswig–Holstein.

FROM ANONYMITY TO HISTORY: SETTLEMENTS IN THE EARLY MEDIEVAL PERIOD

Propitious natural conditions enabled the renewed habitation of the sea marshes in Schleswig–Holstein from the middle of the seventh and eighth centuries onwards. The height of the storm floods at the time of new habitation must have been somewhat lower than before, as ground level settlements were erected on high tidal creek banks in the sea marshes. These conditions can only have been of a short duration because *Wurten* were built from the ninth century. Botanical investigations of some of these settlements demonstrate that extremely halophytic conditions existed around the area at the mouth of the River Eider and in Dithmarschen during the Viking Age, and the *Wurten* were surrounded by salt marsh vegetation.[24] In the early medieval period, the clay marshes of the North Sea area became part of a cultural maritime landscape. The early medieval inhabitation of the wetlands in Schleswig–Holstein is connected with Saxonian and Frisian tribes. In the *Gesta*, by Adams von Bremen, the coastal area of Dithmarschen is described as part of Saxony: '*Transalbianorum Saxonum populi sunt tres. Primi ad oceanum sunt Tedmarsgoi, et eorum ecclesia mater in Melindor*'. The Dithmarscher was one of the three North Elbeian Saxon tribes conquered by Charlemagne in 798. The other two were the Stormarn and Holsten. Three castles, the Bökelnburg and Kuden in the south and the Stellerburg in the north of Dithmarschen, protected this area against enemies (Figure 4). Excavations indicate that the Stellerburg and the Kuden existed in the ninth century.

North of the River Eider, the habitation of the wetlands in the eighth century was often thought to be the result of Frisian immigration. Historical references, however, give no direct information regarding this migration. Archaeological finds, the so-called shell ceramics (*Muschelgruskeramik*) are typical of the Frisian coastal area from the Ijzelmeer to the Weser, but are also found in the coastal areas which are inhabited by Saxon tribes. For example, in ninth century Wellinghusen, the *Muschelgruskeramik* level is lower than in Elisenhof,[25] north of the River Eider, which is a so-called Frisian immigration settlement.

During the occupation of new land which did not begin before the middle of the seventh century, the young marine marshes with their extended salt meadows were populated. In the southern part of Dithmarschen, early medieval settlements are known from the same coastal area as those in Roman times, whereas, in the northern part of Dithmarschen, the Viking age settlements are situated to the west of the Roman settlements. By AD 500, large parts of the Roman period salt marsh had become swampy and peat had developed. In the southern part of the Dithmarschen coastal area, the peat zone is older and has covered the whole lower marsh area since pre-Roman times.

The early medieval *Dorfwurten*, situated in a long line from the mouth of the River Elbe to the River Eider, represent some of the largest and highest in Schleswig–Holstein, which are more than 250 m in diameter and reach heights of MSL +6.20 m (Figure 4). Several of these *Wurten* have been recorded. One of these, the *Wurt* Fahrstedt, near Marne, with finds from the Viking period, was partly destroyed in the nineteenth century.[26] In 1994, extended excavations of a *Wurten* at Wellinghusen, in the northern marsh area of Dithmarschen, unearthed a flat-settlement on a MSL +1.80 m high marsh area along a tidal creek, in which *phragmites* grow (Figures 4, 5). The partly excavated houses, which included possible living quarters and stables, were built on sod mounds encircled by trenches. One of the oldest was erected in AD 691. Increasing storm surges apparently forced the settlers to raise their farmyards after AD 764/820 to 3 m above mean sea level, using manure carefully covered with clay sods. One of these farm buildings – a large stable-house with wickerwork walls – was excavated. In the course of the extension of the house *Wurten*, the tidal creek was filled with dung. A bridge across this creek was still standing

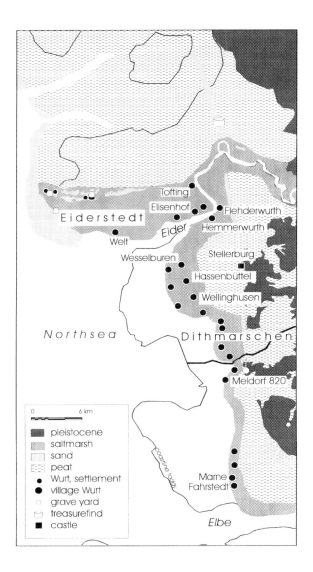

Figure 4 Coastal area of Dithmarschen and Eiderstedt in the early medieval period (AD 700–1000).

in AD 785 (Figure 5). The house *Wurten* were consolidated to form a large *Dorfwurt* during the further expansion of the settlement in the early Middle Ages, reaching an elevation of MSL +3.80 to MSL +4.00 m in the tenth century. From this settlement phase, a smaller building, possibly belonging to a craftsman, has been excavated. Four-row barley (*Hordeum vulgare*), flax (*Linum usitatissimum*) and some cultivated oats (*Avena*) were grown around the *Wurt*. In the high or late medieval period, the settlement was abandoned.

In the tenth century new settlements were founded in the surrounding marsh area. One example is the *Dorfwurt* of Hassenbüttel, 2000 m north of Wellinghusen. The population of a low, often flooded marsh with a height of MSL +0.80 m demanded the erection of *Wurten* with clay and dung layers.[27,28] On one of these *Wurten*, which reach a height of MSL +3.00 m, a large stable-house was erected in the tenth/eleventh centuries. Buildings with sod walls are also documented in this period.

North of the River Eider, the excavated *Dorfwurten* from Elisenhof[29] and Welt[30] are normally connected with the Frisian inhabitation in the eighth century (Figure 4). A number of Viking settlements and burials have been located in Eiderstedt, the larger *Wurten* on the banks of the River Eider, the smaller settlements and grave yards on the old sandy beach ridges. The landward marshes and the northern part of the peninsula were not suitable for settlement as the former were mainly boggy, and the latter was frequently flooded by the sea. On high clay ridges, several farms were built as surface-level settlements with yards which were slowly raised e.g. the site of Elisenhof which has been the subject of intensive archaeological investigations[31] The lower marsh area at Welt soon forced the settlers to build high dwelling mounds.[32] Animal husbandary was the economic base of the settlements, as farming was only possible on a modest scale.

In the inner part of the North Frisian Wadden Sea unfavourable environmental conditions with large peat and swampy areas prevented any habitation before AD 1000. Only the Pleistocene Geest and later partly flooded sea marsh areas were inhabited. A number of settlements and burials are recorded on the Pleistocene deposits of the islands of Amrum, Föhr and Sylt. The edge of the Pleistocene area was densely populated. Nothing is known about the North Frisian sea marsh in spite of the fact that the marsh was inhabited before large areas were flooded over and destroyed in late medieval times. Archaeological finds are known from the western part of the Wadden Sea area, like the tidal area around Hooge and the island of Pellworm. Excavations during the 'Norderhever-Project' have pointed out a flat settlement of the ninth century which was flooded over in the Middle Ages.[33] By this time, the sea level had risen so far that people could no longer live in houses built on top of the land surface, because the marsh was too often flooded during storm tides. *Warften* had, therefore, to be built in Pellworm. Another Viking settlement is known from the Wiedingharde, part of the old North Frisian salt marsh.

Figure 5 Wellinghusen, Dithmarschen. Profile of the early medieval dwelling mound with dung and clay layers, tidal creek (Priel) and house around AD 1000 (Kleinbau).

59

THE FORMING OF THE CULTURAL LANDSCAPE: THE HIGH AND LATE MEDIEVAL PERIODS

The defensive resistance of man against the encroaching sea, expressed by the construction of *Wurten*, was replaced after AD 1000. From the beginning of the eleventh century, dykes were built and the land was drained. The dykes were not, however, high enough to protect the land against the high storm floods. From the high medieval period, the whole area of the sea and river marshes was intensively cultivated and was more densely populated than ever before. New sea marshes – like those in the northern part of Eiderstedt – were inhabited, and the landward swampy areas were drained. Population growth, together with prospering agriculture which enabled levels of food production that surpassed the needs of the farmers themselves, made the establishment of towns possible.

The initiative for the construction of dykes was generally taken by the local people. Economic associations of high social standing organized as co-operatives, developed on village *Warften*, maintaining complete independence from outside nobles and landlords until the late Middle Ages, in Dithmarschen until 1559. The wealth of the leading families was based on the systematic drainage and colonization of the inland marshes and bogs, which created the transition from a natural landscape to the present-day cultivated landscape.

Large dyke systems stretching along larger parts of the Dithmarschen coast and the south part of Eiderstedt were built jointly by these groups and the local administrations organised in church areas (Figure 6). The co-operatives themselves decided on the location, and the method of construction and maintenance of the dykes, channels and sluices. In the newly drained areas the farms of the settlers, built on little single dwelling mounds for protection from the inland waters, were drawn across the landscape like beads on a string, their narrow strips of fields penetrating farther and farther into the bogs.

High *Warften* of clay were erected on the low marshes of northern Eiderstedt and the seaward area of the modern North Frisian Wadden Sea, where island-like patches were separated by numerous tidal creeks. Their names are Stufhusen, Sieversfleth, Helmfleth and Hundorf. Even today they still determine the appearence of the landscape in Westerhever, and around Osterhever and Poppenbüll. The *Warften* were suddenly raised because salt water often inundated the low marsh. Excavations in Hundorf have documented a twelfth century-dwelling mound with a height of MSL +3.00 m, which was raised to MSL +4.00 m in the fourteenth century.[34,35] The *Warft* was built with clay in the twelfth century and expanded at the edges with some manure and more clay. The family and co-operative groups of these *Warften*, largely independent of superior authorities and organised into parishes, began to erect dykes to protect their cultivated lands, in which single *Warften* were built. The best remaining example of this medieval landscape

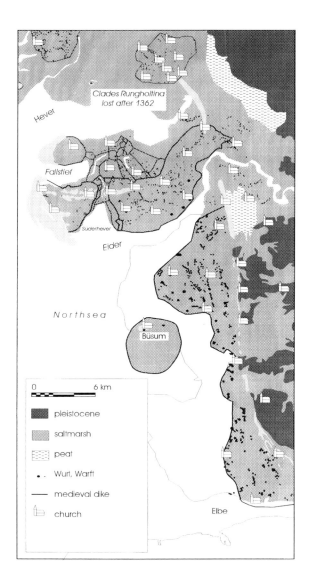

Text visible within the map:

Clades Rungholtina
lost after 1362

Hever

Fallstief

Suderhever

Eider

North sea

Büsum

Elbe

0   6 km

pleistocene
saltmarsh
peat
Wurt, Warft
medieval dike
church

Figure 6 Dithmarschen and Eiderstedt in the high and late medieval periods (AD 1000–1400).

is the polder of St. Johannis (Figure 7). The surrounding low summer dyke, excavated with two trenches, was MSL +1.50 m in the twelfth century and was raised further in the late Middle Ages.

To the west and north-west, this dyke borders on the wide Fallstief, which was not dammed until the mid-fifteenth century; to the east it borders the polder of Iversbüller Koog, a sea dyke built into Offenbüll Bay, which had been reclaimed by the sea and was not dyked until early modern times. With the construction of higher dykes since the late medieval period, the overflow space for high storm floods was reduced as the dykes offered complete protection against the sea. The more recent dykes built by order of feudal authorities are characterised by greater height and straight lines which no longer follow natural landscape structures.

Nordfriesland (Uthlande) suffered great losses of land during the late Middle Ages and in early modern times. During the storm floods of 1362 and 1634, a large part of the Uthlande of North Frisia between Eiderstedt in the south and the island of Sylt in the north was completely lost (Figure 8). The salt marsh areas, which had been occupied and cultivated by man since the Viking period, became part of the tidal flats because the surface was situated lower than MHW. The reasons for these catastrophes are partly due to geological development and partly to the activity of man. Local factors have to be considered in time and space when interpreting landscape development. In the course of the fourteenth century, the sea permanently flooded the North Frisian salt marshes. Those areas especially affected were those in which the compaction of sediments had happened before. It is, therefore, obvious that the sea did not break into these areas as a consequence of sediment compaction.

Another factor of the land losses in the Middle Ages was the extensive cutting of the salt peat, which often left the surface lower than MHW. The sediment-covered peat was cut and burned, and the salt absorbed in the peat was sold as 'Frisian salt'. As a result of these measures, reclamation of flooded land after dyke breaks was often impossible. Nowadays the remains of medieval settlements are frequently found in the tidal flat area.

CONCLUSION

The central themes of the coastal archaeology in Schleswig–Holstein are the reconstruction of coastal development, environment and settlement. The fieldwork programme concentrates first on the excavation of dwelling mounds and since the seventies, on the reconstruction of the landscape and the settlement history of larger areas. Within mapping of the cultural elements of the coastal area, integrated programmes of archaeological, geological and palaeobotanical survey were undertaken on the island of Sylt, in the North Frisian Wadden Sea, Eiderstedt and Dithmarschen.

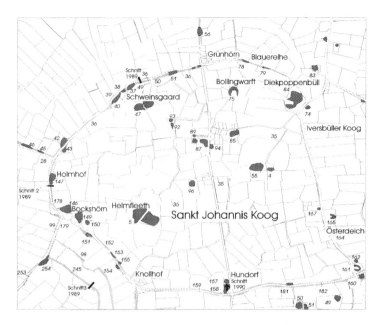

Figure 7 St. Johannis Koog Polder, Eiderstedt. Medieval Ring dyke and dwelling mounds.

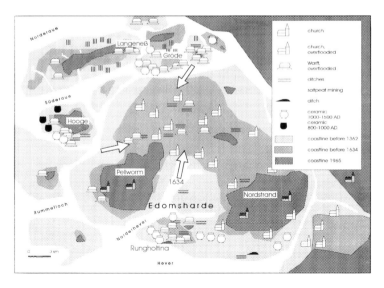

Figure 8 Land losses in southern North Frisia from 1362 until 1634.

63

The results of these investigations are that the environmental changes dominate the settlement history and the settlement pattern in the first millenium AD. After dyking and draining, the natural landscape changes to a cultural landscape. Archaeological finds and excavations have pointed out that the salt marshes of Schleswig–Holstein were not occupied until the early Roman period. The settlements were founded in the salt marshes near to the sea and in general away from the peat zones. The river marshes and the sea marshes in Dithmarschen and in the south part of Eiderstedt were densely populated. The habitation of the sea marsh in the first and second centuries took place in a phase of lowering sea level. Ground place settlements could be founded on high clay deposits. The renewed activity of the sea again caused flooding, and some settlements had to be abandoned or the inhabitants protected themselves against the storm floods with the construction of *Wurten*. The largest *Wurten* – like Tofting – contain several layers of habitation.

After the migration period new settlements, later *Wurten*, were founded in Dithmarschen and Eiderstedt. Typical examples – like Wellinghusen, Hassenbüttel, Elisenhof and Welt – are represented in this article. The present North Frisian Wadden Sea was covered with peat, and could be not inhabited before the high medieval period. Viking Age settlements are only known from the western part of the Wadden Sea, like the island of Pellworm and the tidal area around Hooge.

During the high medieval period, the natural landscape changes to a cultural landscape. Co-operatives of peasants and the church played an important role in the development of the coastal area: dykes were built and the lower ground areas were drained and cultivated. Catastrophic storm floods in the late medieval period had a terrible effect: a large part of the North Frisian Uthlande was destroyed by the sea.

Cultural monuments relating to coastal history remain in the landscape today. The protection of the cultural heritage is of great importance for the future. A working programme – based on the mapping of cultural heritage – has, therefore, been founded by the European Union (LANCEWAD – Landscape and Cultural Heritage of the Wadden Sea).

References

1.   *Trilateral Wadden Sea Plan 1997: Stade Declaration, Ministerial Declaration of the Eighth Trilateral Governmental Conference on the Protection of the Wadden Sea*, 1998.

2.   Bantelmann, A., *Tofting, eine vorgeschichtliche Warft an der Eidermündung*, Offa-Bücher 12, 1955.

3.   Bantelmann, A., *Die frühgeschichtliche Marschensiedlung beim Elisenhof in Eiderstedt. Landschaftsgeschichte und Baubefunde*, Studien Küstenarchäologie Schleswig-Holstein A, Elisenhof 1, 1975.

4. Müller-Wille, M. et al, *Norderhever-Projekt. 1 Landschaftsentwicklung und Siedlungsgeschichte im Einzugsgebiet der Norderhever (Nordfriesland)*, Offa-Bücher 66, Studien Küstenarchäologie Schleswig-Holstein C, Norderhever 1, 1988.

5. Hoffmann, D. et al, 'Geologische und archäologische Untersuchungen zur Landschafts- und Siedlungsgeschichte des Küstengebietes von Norderdithmarschen', in *Germania* 75, 1997, pp. 213–253.

6. Meier, D., 'Landschaftsgeschichte, Siedlungs- und Wirtschaftsweise der Marsch', in Verein f. Dithmarscher Landeskunde (ed), *Geschichte Dithmarschens*, Heide, 2000, pp. 71–92.

7. Ehlers, J., *The morphodynamics of the Wadden Sea*, Rotterdam-Brookfield, 1988.

8. Behre, K.-E., *Die Pflanzenreste aus der frühgeschichtlichen Wurt Elisenhof*, Studien Küstenarchäologie Schleswig–Holstein A, Elisenhof 2, 1976.

9. Harck, O., 'Landschaftsgeschichte und Archäologie an der Westküste der jütischen Halbinsel', in Kossack, G. et al, *Archsum auf Sylt*, Teil 1, Stud. Küstenarchäologie Schleswig-Holstein B, Archsum 1 = Röm.-Germ. Forsch. 39, 1980, pp. 32–63.

10. Lübke, H., 'Fedderingen-Wurth, ein Fundplatz der Ertebölle/Ellerbek-Kultur', in Drenkhahn, D. et al (ed), *Frühe Siedler an der Küste, Küstenarchäologie in Dithmarschen und Steinburg*, Heide, 1991, pp. 38–46.

11. Arnold, V., 'Ur- und Frühgeschichte', in Verein f. Dithmarscher Landeskunde (ed), *Geschichte Dithmarschens*, Heide, 2000, pp. 17–70.

12. Ibid., p. 27ff.

13. Hingst, H., *Die vorrömische Eisenzeit Westholsteins*, Offa-Bücher 49, 1983.

14. Ibid., p. 74.

15. Haarnagel, W., 'Die Marschensiedlungen in Schleswig-Holstein und im linkselbischen Küstengebiet', in *Probleme der Küstenforschung 1*, 1940, pp. 87–98.

16. Bantelmann, A., 'Die kaiserzeitliche Marschensiedlung von Ostermoor bei Brunsbüttelkoog', in *Offa* 16, 1957/58, pp. 53–79.

17. Bantelmann, A., *Tofting, eine vorgeschichtliche Warft an der Eidermündung*, Offa-Bücher 12, 1955.

18. Behre, K.-E., *Die Pflanzenreste aus der frühgeschichtlichen Wurt Elisenhof*, Studien Küstenarchäologie Schleswig-Holstein A, Elisenhof 2, 1976.

19. Bantelmann, A., *Tofting, eine vorgeschichtliche Warft an der Eidermündung*, Offa-Bücher 12, 1955.

20. Bantelmann, A., 'Spuren vor- und frühgeschichtlicher Besiedlung auf einem Strandwall bei Tating, Eiderstedt', in *Probleme der Küstenforschung* 9, 1970, pp. 49–55.

21. Müller-Wille, D., 'Frühgeschichtliche Fundplätze in Eiderstedt', in *Offa* 43, 1986, pp. 295–310.

22. Hoffmann, D. et al, 'Geologische und archäologische Untersuchungen zur Landschafts- und Siedlungsgeschichte des Küstengebietes von Norderdithmarschen', in *Germania,* 75, 1997, pp. 213–253.

23.   Meier, D., 'Landschaftsgeschichte und Siedlungsmuster von der römischen Kaiserzeit bis in das Mittelalter in den Küstengebieten Eiderstedts und Dithmarschens. Siedlungsforschung', in *Archäologie – Geschichte – Geographie,* 14, 1996, pp. 245–276.

24.   Behre, K.-E., *Die Pflanzenreste aus der frühgeschichtlichen Wurt Elisenhof.* Studien Küstenarchäologie Schleswig–Holstein A, Elisenhof 2, 1976.

25.   Steuer, H., *Die Keramik aus der frühgeschichtlichen Warft Elisenhof,* Studien Küstenarchäologie Schleswig–Holstein A, Elisenhof 3, 1979.

26.   Hartmann, R., *Die alten Dithmarscher Wurten und ihr Packwerkbau,* Marne, 1883.

27.   Hoffmann, D. et al, 'Geologische und archäologische Untersuchungen zur Landschafts- und Siedlungsgeschichte des Küstengebietes von Norderdithmarschen', in *Germania,* 75, 1997, pp. 213–253.

28.   Meier, D., 'Transalbianorum Saxonum populi sunt tres. Das Dithmarscher Küstengebiet im frühen und hohen Mittelalter', in Wesse, A. (Hrsg), *Studien zur Archäologie des Ostseeraumes. Von der Eisenzeit zum Mittelalter. Festschrift M. Müller-Wille,* Neumünster, 1988, pp. 77–90.

29.   Bantelmann, A., *Die frühgeschichtliche Marschensiedlung beim Elisenhof in Eiderstedt. Landschaftsgeschichte und Baubefunde,* Studien Küstenarchäologie Schleswig-Holstein A, Elisenhof 1, 1975.

30.   Meier, D., 'Welt, eine frühmittelalterliche Dorfwurt im Mündungsgebiet der Eider', in *Archäologisches Korrespondenzblatt,* 27, 1997, pp. 171–184.

31.   Bantelmann, A., 'Die frühgeschichtliche Marschensiedlung beim Elisenhof', in *Eiderstedt. Landschaftsgeschichte und Baubefunde,* Studien Küstenarchäologie Schleswig–Holstein A, Elisenhof 1, 1975.

32.   Meier, D., 'Welt, eine frühmittelalterliche Dorfwurt im Mündungsgebiet der Eider', in *Archäologisches Korrespondenzblatt,* 27, 1997, pp. 171–184.

33.   Müller-Wille, M. et al, *Norderhever-Projekt. 1 Landschaftsentwicklung und Siedlungsgeschichte im Einzugsgebiet der Norderhever (Nordfriesland),* Offa-Bücher 66, Studien Küstenarchäologie Schleswig–Holstein C, Norderhever 1, 1988.

34.   Meier, D., 'Landschaftsgeschichte und Siedlungsmuster von der römischen Kaiserzeit bis in das Mittelalter in den Küstengebieten Eiderstedts und Dithmarschens. Siedlungsforschung', in *Archäologie – Geschichte – Geographie,* 14, 1996, pp. 245–276.

35.   Meier, D. et al, 'Zum mittelalterlichen Landesausbau Eiderstedts. Ein Forschungsprojekt der Arbeitsgruppe Küstenarchäologie, Forschungs- und Technologiezentrum Büsum', in *Offa* 46, 1989, pp. 285–300.

Further Reading

Behre, K.-E., 'Die Umwelt prähistorischer und mittelalterlicher Siedlungen. Siedlungsforschung', in *Archäologie – Geschichte – Geographie 6,* 1988, pp. 57–80.

Haarnagel, W., 'Die Ergebnisse der Grabung auf der ältereisenzeitlichen Siedlung Boomborg/Hatzum, Kreis Leer, in den Jahren von 1965 bis 1967', in *Neue*

Ausgrabungen und Forschungen in Niedersachsen 4, 1969, pp. 2–44.

Haarnagel, W., *Die Grabung Feddersen Wierde. Methode, Hausbau, Siedlungs- und Wirtschaftsformen sowie Sozialstruktur*, 1979.

Kossack, G. et al, *Archäologische und naturwissenschaftliche Untersuchungen an ländlichen und frühstädtischen Siedlungen im deutschen Küstengebiet vom 5. Jahrhundert n.Chr. bis zum 11. Jahrhundert n.Chr. 1 Ländliche Siedlungen*, Weinheim, 1984.

Knol, E., *De Nordnederlandse kustlanden in de Vroege Middeleeuwen*, 1993.

7

PLANARCH
Archaeology and Planning around the Southern North Sea Basin

John Williams

Planarch is an Interreg IIC project for the North-West Metropolitan Area which draws together five regions in four countries around the southern North Sea Basin. Particular attention is being paid within the project to:

- investigating methodologies for field evaluation of archaeological sites, especially for major infrastructure projects and in relation to alluvial sequences
- incorporating archaeological information and associated policies within the spatial planning process
- developing common data standards to enable free exchange of digital information across the project area
- generally taking forward best practice in archaeology and planning.

THE BIRTH OF THE PROJECT

Increasingly over the last few years there has been more co-operation between archaeologists around the southern North Sea Basin. Kent and Essex have been working together on a Research Framework for the Greater Thames Estuary and Kent and Nord-Pas de Calais have been involved in an Interreg IIA project related to historic fortifications. More widely, professional contact networks were being established through the European Association of Archaeologists, and the establishment of a Euroregion involving Kent, Nord-Pas de Calais and the three Belgian regions, was helping to foster partnership working in areas such as planning and economic development.

The region is one which is subject to great development pressure, including major infrastructure works, such as the Channel Tunnel Rail Link in Kent, Stansted Airport in Essex, major harbour works at Antwerp in Belgium and Rotterdam in the Netherlands and industrial development around Valenciennes in northern France. It was clear that individually and collectively archaeologists and planners in the regions where such activity was taking place could learn a lot from each other, both in terms of fieldwork and professional best practice and in the better integration of archaeological resource management within the planning process. As a result Planarch was born, bringing together a diverse range of partners from around the southern North Sea Basin: Kent County Council (as lead partner), Essex County Council, the Regional Archaeological Service for Nord-Pas de Calais, the University of Ghent, the Province of East Flanders, the Wallonian Archaeological Service, the Dutch Archaeological Service, the Province of South Holland and the Muncipality of Rotterdam.

The project was born out of a desire to work together on common problems. Indeed the seeds of co-operation were sown before a vehicle for taking things forward was identified. The area of common ground related very much to cultural resource management, although the different partners inevitably had different emphases which might be more academically, technically or planning orientated. The Interreg IIC programme seemed to provide an excellent framework, being essentially based in spatial planning. There were difficulties, however, not least the division of competences within the individual regions and countries, the varying levels of integration of archaeology within spatial planning, and the different legislative and administrative structures. The Secretariat for the North-West Metropolitan Area Programme also needed to be convinced about what was specifically trans-frontier about archaeological resource management in general and in relation to the Planarch project. A unifying influence, however, was the ongoing assimilation of the principles of the Valetta Convention by the various partner organisations: archaeological heritage management was increasingly an issue of the moment across the region.

THE PLANARCH METHOD OF WORKING

Underpinning the project was, on the one hand, a desire to undertake real archaeological work and, on the other, to exchange experience and best practice. Linking all was the will to integrate archaeology further within spatial planning processes and generally raise standards of archaeological resource management. A steering group was formed with two representatives from each region (England, France, Flanders, Wallonia and the Netherlands) supported by a half-time project administrator based with the lead partner (experience has since shown that a complex project such as Planarch warrants such an officer being full-time). Most partners are responsible for pilot demonstration actions which have real benefit to their own region and also develop best practice more generally. In addition there are a number of joint actions which encourage collective working and develop common understanding. This collaboration has been reinforced by joint seminars and exchanges of personnel.

THE PROJECT IN ACTION

The project has eight main areas of work, which will now be reviewed in turn. Since, however, the project is still ongoing at the time of writing, this is inevitably an interim statement.

1. Establishing an active partnership
The establishment of an active partnership was absolutely essential if the other actions within the project were to be taken forward efficiently and effectively. The steering group plays a key role here, but others attend meetings as and when relevant. An attempt is made at most meetings to look at real issues on the ground as a sound basis for exchanging experience and best practice. This, however, is very much reinforced by the programme of exchanges taking place between members of the various partner organisations, where such different areas as field techniques, SMR development, GIS techniques and approaches to spatial planning are covered.

2. Reviewing organisational structures for archaeology
Across the Planarch area the organisational frameworks for archaeology are complex, with the state and the various levels of regional and local administration having somewhat different roles in each of the partner regions, reflecting national approaches to government. A better understanding of the various frameworks inevitably assists joint working and the issues were examined in a series of papers at the first Planarch seminar held in Maidstone in May 2000.[1]

In England the role of the private consultant and contractor is now well developed, mirroring successive governments' philosophy as to the role of the private sector and indeed the rights and responsibilities of the individual, whereas elsewhere greater emphasis seems to be placed on the collective ownership of the past. There is also variation in the application of developer funding and the principle of 'polluter pays' across the region. Again the position of the volunteer and the strength of national and local societies varies from country to country and from region to region. The relationship between archaeologist and planner has been increasingly recognised in recent years, and the principles contained within the Valetta Convention, and more generally related to the concept of sustainability, have led to the need to rethink how the historic environment should be safeguarded and managed in relation to development pressures. This can be most vividly seen in the Netherlands where there is currently a re-structuring of archaeological organisational frameworks to take account of the evolving thinking. How archaeology is integrated in planning, however, varies. In some areas, notably England, archaeologists, working alongside other environmental specialists, are part of planning departments; whereas, elsewhere, specialist services are more compartmentalised or independent of the planning system, though linked to it. There is, however, increasing awareness in all the partner regions of the need for better integration of archaeology and spatial planning.

3. Reviewing legislative and planning frameworks

Again, understanding of legal and planning frameworks of the various regions assists in the taking forward of an effective partnership. It also helps the development of best practice. The issues here were examined in the second Planarch seminar held at Mons in November 2000.[2]

A common factor was the increasing influence of European directives, such as the Environmental Impact Assessment regulations, and conventions such as the Valetta Convention on cultural resource management and the Florence Convention on landscapes. The principles of these conventions are influencing evolving philosophies across the region, and indeed the Netherlands is changing its archaeological infrastructure to bring it more closely into line with the Convention.

Across the region major infrastructure projects undertaken by government or quasi-governmental bodies are subject to a formal planning process and the principle of developer funding. For smaller development projects the situation is more varied. While in England archaeologists may be more integrated in planning and developer funding is applicable to even the smallest of developments, elsewhere archaeologists, based within regional or national governmental organisations, perhaps have more direct power, being more independent of local planning committees.

4. Developing information exchange on the common cultural heritage

One of the underlying concepts of the Planarch project was that of the southern North Sea Basin as an historic cultural entity. About 8,500 years ago England was joined to mainland Europe and the Thames, the Rhine, the Meuse and the Scheldt formed part of a single river system emptying into a common estuary. Subsequently the southern North Sea has acted both as a means of communication for intellectual exchange and material trade and as a highway for more hostile intent. However, it has also been a barrier both to cultural and aggressive action. The Basin thus seems to have an archaeological and historical coherence, but the interactions between the peoples around its shores need to be examined further. Planarch has a role in developing understanding of this common heritage. Wherever possible, Planarch partners have used the opportunity to exchange information on the archaeology of the region and this has been integrated into all the seminars. This exchange of information has a clear academic value but is also invaluable in developing and strengthening a sense of purpose within the project partnership.

5. Developing integration and networking of information
Central to developing an archaeological overview of the region, whether for purely academic reasons or alternatively for those of heritage resource management, is an ability to exchange information. The modern computer world offers both challenges and opportunities. An objective of the project, therefore, was to look at Sites and Monuments Records and similar across the project area, with a view to implementing, if possible, core data standards which would facilitate digital exchange of at least a selected range of information. It has been interesting to compare the different data frameworks within the partner regions, although the basic concepts are the same, even though there is still debate over the fundamental question of what constitutes a site. All the partners are using GIS to greater or lesser degrees, thus emphasising the central role which computerised mapping has to play in archaeology and spatial planning. If we are to recognise a 'common heritage', the ability to exchange information easily is important.

6. Developing archaeological and planning decision-making
This is a key area of the project and is being taken forward by five linked projects. There is a common thread or problem: rich archaeological deposits, often buried within alluvial deposits of some depth and so not immediately identifiable on the surface, but which are vulnerable to development pressures or natural processes, such as coastal erosion and sea-level change. The projects were intended to look at methodologies for predictive modelling of archaeological potential over broad areas; enhance the knowledge base of the archaeological resource in the respective areas; enhance the analytical capabilities of databases and GIS; and inform spatial planning and other management policy frameworks.

In England the project is looking at areas of the Greater Thames estuary, concentrating on the intertidal areas and the immediate hinterland of the shore. Significant alluvial deposits have built up over the centuries as a result of sea-level change and these are now under threat from coastal erosion. Wessex Archaeology has undertaken a complete revision of the Kent SMR for the coastal area, enhancing both the database and the associated GIS.[3] This is a prelude to systematic field validation. In Essex selected areas are being investigated in the field. All this work will lead to a greater understanding of the archaeology of the Greater Thames Estuary and, hopefully, its more effective management.

In the Netherlands the area of Voorne-Putten, to the south of Rotterdam, is the subject of another pilot study. Here the expansion of the port is a major concern. The lowering of the water table and fragmentation of the landscape, through major development works, are posing an immediate and longer-term threat to the archaeological resource. Given the reclaimed nature of much of the Dutch landscape, archaeological levels are often buried beneath greater or lesser depths of alluvial build-up. Attention is being paid in the project to the use of borehole surveys for archaeological predictive modelling. Another study is monitoring the level of the water table and the quality of the water relating to a Neolithic site which has been preserved *in situ* in open space within a housing development. It will be interesting to see whether preservation *in situ* is a real long-term option in such cases.

Similarly the Belgian port of Antwerp is undergoing considerable expansion and this will have a considerable impact on the buried archaeological landscape of the area. It is again a reclaimed landscape with a substantial alluvial build-up. The University of Ghent is undertaking a systematic programme of boreholing and at the same time monitoring the massive earthmoving associated with the construction of new harbours. The idea is to draw an archaeological map, which can be used as a reliable basis for planning policies for the area.

The Nord-Pas de Calais and Wallonian Archaeological Services are collaborating in developing comprehensive archaeological mapping for the valley of the Escaut, which runs across the border between France and Belgium. It is again an area subject to major development pressure and the project will hopefully be instrumental in embedding archaeological policies within the development framework.

The work is being carried out in the respective areas by teams from the individual countries and there is continuous assessment and exchange of knowledge and experience of the various partners before, during and after the projects. Importantly there is also an ongoing series of exchanges of personnel between the various regions, with special attention being paid to learning from the strengths and weaknesses of the various participating organisations.

In all of these projects the key perspective is one of long term management of the archaeological resource, and for this the involvement of planners and other land-use specialists is required. In order to achieve lasting solutions, archaeologists must justify themselves not only to themselves but also to society at large.

7. Reviewing archaeological assessment and evaluation techniques

With archaeology now much more a consideration in the planning process and the cost of archaeological mitigation being high, whether it is funded by developers or national or local government, there is an increasing need for effective assessment of the archaeological potential of a given site. Techniques employed should be both academically reliable and cost effective. Consideration of this area of work is central to the project, particularly the pilot studies discussed above, but provision was also made in the project for a more detailed consideration of the issues. Most of the partners had been involved in large scale infrastructure projects where it was possible to compare what was predicted in evaluation with what was actually found. Indeed it is only by completing the circle and reviewing the effectiveness of what was actually done that all the lessons can be learnt. Part of the Maidstone seminar was devoted to a consideration of the issues, with particular attention being paid to field evaluation utilising boreholing and trial trenching.[4]

In addition a detailed study was undertaken by the Oxford Archaeological Unit on some major development sites, primarily in Kent and Essex, where large areas had been stripped.[5] In addition to looking generally at the effectiveness of the sampling strategies actually employed, computer simulations considered the effect, for trial trenching, of using different trench arrays and different percentage coverages. As might be expected it was shown that it is easier to detect sites with large quantities of artefacts where there are large numbers of archaeological features, particularly continuous ditches. It is much more difficult to locate sites comprising a limited number of dispersed elements, particularly for periods where there are fewer artefacts. Thus in an English context it is much easier to find late Iron Age, Roman and Medieval sites than Neolithic, Bronze Age and Anglo-Saxon sites. Of equal significance was the fact that 2% sampling is unreliable, that 10% is, under most conditions, effective, and that 5% is perhaps the most cost effective. Whereas up to 5% there is a fairly standard increase in predictive accuracy in relation to cost, above 5% the law of diminishing returns begins to apply. There are certainly lessons to be learnt.

8. Promoting best practice
The partners recognised that the project would only have limited value if it was undertaken by archaeologists for archaeologists. If, as the Valetta Convention states, the archaeological heritage is a 'source of the European collective memory', it is important that it is valued by all. A first step is to develop more effective archaeological resource management and for this the various studies and pieces of work being undertaken by the project are being published. In addition six copies of a portable trilingual exhibition have been made. The exhibition looks at the nature of the archaeological resource within the project area and how it should be effectively managed. It is aimed at planners and the general public. More generally there is an attempt to make the project and its outcomes widely known.

CONCLUSION

The Planarch project is important for a number of reasons. It is making a real contribution to developing understanding of archaeology and archaeological processes across the region covered by the project; it is helping to set new standards for archaeological resource management; and, not least, within a programme set up for interregional partnerships, it is both bringing archaeologists, planners and others together across the region and also showing the relevance of archaeology to society at large.

THE PLANARCH PARTNERS

Kent County Council (lead partner)
Essex County Council
ROB-Rijksdienst voor het Oudheidkundig Bodemonderzoek, the Netherlands
The Province of South Holland, The Netherlands
BOOR-Bureau Oudheidkundig Onderzoek Rotterdam, the Netherlands
Service de l'Archéologie, Province de Hainaut, Wallonia, Belgium
The Province of East Flanders, Belgium
The University of Ghent, Belgium
DRAC-Direction Régionale des Affaires Culturelles, Nord - Pas de Calais, Service Régionale de l'Archéologie, France

References

1. Evans, K. and Williams, J.H., *The Organisation of Archaeology in England, Belgium (Flanders & Wallonia), France and the Netherlands*, 2001.
2. Evans, K. and Williams, J.H., *The Legislative Framework for Archaeology in England, Belgium (Flanders & Wallonia), France and the Netherlands*, forthcoming.
3. Wessex Archaeology, *Historic Environment of the North Kent Coast Rapid Coastal Zone Assessment Survey; Survey Phase 1 Final Report*, 2000.
4. Evans, K. and Williams, J.H., *Approaches to Archaeological Evaluation in England, Belgium (Flanders & Wallonia), France and the Netherlands*, forthcoming.
5. Hey, G., *Evaluation of Archaeological Decision-making Processes and Sampling Strategies*, 2001.

8

SUSTAINABLE DEVELOPMENT IN THE HISTORICAL CENTRE OF RIBE, DENMARK
As Seen from the Point of View of the Museum

Jakob Kieffer-Olsen

As a result of archaeological investigations, Ribe currently holds the title of 'The oldest town in Denmark'. It is not very old, however, when compared to countries which have a Roman past. Excavations have shown that there has been continuous occupation combined with market activity and trade since the beginning of the eighth century. The basis of the town was trade with the countries around the North Sea: present day Germany; the Netherlands; Belgium; France; England; Scotland, and Norway. In particular, trade-routes from the areas to the south and south-west of Ribe went to this part of Jutland, and from here goods were transported eastwards by water in small river-boats or across land to the harbours on the south-east coast of Jutland. This traffic formed the basis of towns such as Hedeby/Slesvig and Ribe.[1]

Christian monks and priests came to this area when they began their mission in Denmark, and in the 850s Ansgar was given permission to build churches in Hedeby and Ribe. It was to be more than 100 years, however, before Christianity was accepted by the Danes (Figure 1).[2]

International trade continued to pass through the south of Jutland. In the thirteenth century, the development of ships, navigation and knowledge of the sea made it possible for greater numbers of trading-ships to pass through the dangerous waters to the west and north of Jutland. As time went on more and more of the international trade passed by Ribe, and by the end of the seventeenth century the town was simply a regional harbour. In 1868 the

Figure 1   The eighth-century market place in Ribe. *Drawing: Flemming Bau*

Danish state decided that a modern west-coast harbour was needed and Esbjerg was chosen, thereby ending Ribe's involvement in anything other than local trade.[3]

Until the end of the seventeenth century, Ribe was one of the biggest towns in Denmark, and it was possibly the biggest before 1300. Today it is a small local town with less than 10,000 inhabitants.

Ribe was situated on the north-east bank of the river for approximately 400 years. First a ditch and later a rampart and moat separated the area of the Viking town from the surrounding vicinity. The market-place was located close to the river, whereas domestic buildings and graves were situated more to the east.

The south-west bank of the river was occupied in c. 1100. The twelfth-century cathedral was built here together with parish churches, monasteries, chapels and a hospital. The old part of the town still existed and provided space for additional parish-churches, a monastery, a hospital and a chapel. The town grew, and the demand for new land led to the filling up of parts of the river which became narrower. When the town began to decline, remote areas were given up, and buildings became concentrated in one area. Houses disappeared from both the north-eastern and the far western part of the town, and the royal castle was abandoned (Figure 2).[4]

In present day Ribe, a few of the houses are medieval, many are from the sixteenth and seventeenth centuries, some from the eighteenth and the rest are mainly from the nineteenth century. The old part of the town is still thriving and contains shops such as the bookseller and the hardware-store. The only remaining grocer's shop, however, which is on the main street, now sells wine and specialities, and the major part of the town's daily food-supply has to be bought outside the old town.

Preservation work and plans for sustainable development not only have to consider the archaeological heritage and the buildings worthy of preservation, but they also need to ensure that the old town is kept alive. Another consideration is how to provide information about the historic town for visitors walking around it, without the town becoming an outdoor exhibition.

Much of the archaeological heritage is concealed beneath the present town. To defend against incursions of the North Sea, the citizens of Ribe raised the levels of their building plots. For example, in 1361 and 1636, severe floods hit Ribe and other parts of the Wadden Sea area, causing many casualties. In some areas, where the town is spread out over the old river-bed, the cultural layers are more than 7 m thick. In the rest of the south-western part of the town, the layers are an average of 3–4 m thick, and in the north-eastern part they range from zero to just over a metre. The history of the once very important town of Ribe is hidden in this soil (Figure 3).

The present law protects only small areas of the archaeological heritage. Building remains are not protected even when we know exactly where they are located, as for example the case of medieval monasteries. If somebody

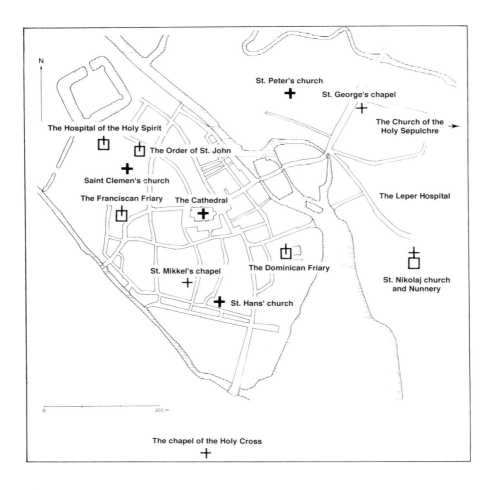

Figure 2 Ribe, just before the Reformation in 1536, with 14 church buildings: chapels hospitals monasteries; parish churches and the cathedral. Only two churches survived the Reformation. (*Nielsen, 1985, p. 46*)

wants to build something and the local authorities have no objections, they can do so without taking the archaeological heritage into consideration. The local museum, however, does carry out archaeological investigations on behalf of the State Antiquarian.

The current law requires that the state has to pay for archaeological excavation if it is caused by a private individual or company. Public companies, communities such as the municipality, the county or the church, have to pay for excavations themselves. This financial situation acts as a break on any public building that will disturb the archaeological heritage, but does not affect private builders. In one place, an excavation took place which cost one million Danish crowns because the builder did not want his parking places to settle. He wanted foundations of sand that went down to the natural soil, a depth of more than 2 m.

The Danish parliament has just passed a new law to preserve the archaeological heritage. Planning has to take archaeology into consideration, the State Antiquarian has the power to stop building projects, and the cost of future archaeological excavations has to be paid by the builder in all cases.

If a builder in Ribe refuses to bear the cost for disturbing the archaeological heritage, he will not be able to build inside the old town. A possible consequence of this, however, might be that building activity could become scarce which might then have a detrimental effect on the life of the old town. With help from colleagues in Norway and Sweden who have experienced this situation for some years, we are trying to encourage people to build on concrete plates which float on top of the cultural layers without disturbing them severely. This will bring the cost of archaeological excavations down to a minimum. At the moment, this possibility is being considered for an area between Præstegade and Grønnegade, two streets where the cultural layers are 5 m thick. A major excavation took place here in 1955, and the remains of many buildings were located (Figure 4).

When it comes to the buildings of the present town, the museum has no authority at all. We are kept informed about developments and asked for advice in some situations, but as we do not have any authority we consequently have no obligations.

A discussion and investigation concerning the level of water in the river is currently taking place as measurements have shown that the level has been lowered. This has been caused by human activities such as straightening out or deepening parts of the river, widening the river, and building the sea dyke. These actions have helped to prevent flooding etc. The lowering of the water level in the river, however, also means that the level of water in the cultural layers has been lowered. If the cultural layers dry out large parts of the town will settle and cause major damage to the buildings. When investigations are completed, it is hoped that the water level in the river can be raised in some way.

Figure 3 In 1993 the sewer in Grønnegade was replaced, and an archaeological investigation took place. In this spot the cultural layers are more than 5 m deep. ©*Hans Skov*

Figure 4 The excavation in 1955 is often referred to as 'Denmark's first modern town-excavation'. The number of objects and building remains was surprisingly large. ©*Den antikvariske Samling*

Turning now to the town-plan, the streets of the old town follow the medieval street plan. We have gained this information through archaeological investigations which took place when work was carried out on the sewers. The streets are curved, so that when you stand at one end, you cannot see the other end. This gives the streets and the town a kind of soul, and allows the viewer to feel that they are discovering something for themselves. In 1875, town planners put one ruler-straight street through the town. This street ran from the railway station to the town hall, crossing the old streets and deforming the plots so that owners were forced to build trapezoidal houses.

The medieval streets are like tunnels in the sense, that the houses line the streets in unbroken rows and any spaces in between are closed with walls or hoardings. The houses are nearly all old, the streets are paved and old-style lamps are used. Thus, the town plan, the streets and the houses form a unity, and walking through the streets gives the impression of stepping back in time. This is not only true of the facades which front onto the streets. The frontages of many of the older timber-framed houses were modernised at the end of the eighteenth or in the nineteenth centuries, whereas the backs were left unaltered.

Accidental fires or the infilling of vacant plots sometimes lead to redevelopment, which potentially challenges the architectural unity of the old town. In order to avoid disturbing the impression of being in the past, the new houses must look like the old ones.

When I discuss this situation with architects, they sometimes express the wish that they were able to design a totally modern prestige building, that could correspond and fit in with the old houses. They feel that this would bring another quality to the town. What they do not see is the fact that a modern house, despite its qualities, will destroy the unity of the old houses. Houses in the modern style are not needed in the old town because there is enough room outside it for this type of architecture.

Periodically a street will need to be repaired or a house modernised. The local authorities involve the museum in their work on the streets. It is intended that most streets will be paved with the possible exception of the main traffic road. The aim is to give each street its own personality, using the already existing variations in paving. The historic elements of the present street equipment will also be kept including horse mounting blocks, drains, and stones which protect the exposed corners of buildings (Figure 5).

There are greater problems with the buildings themselves. Many of the houses are protected by a national preservation scheme, and the rest by a local scheme but nevertheless people have to re-build and modernise their property. Plans for any work has to be approved by the local authorities, with approval also required from the national authorities for preserved houses. Changes have to be acceptable, particularly if they are to be made to the facades or to the original features of the preserved buildings. The majority of the people responsible have an architectural background, so this part of

Figure 5 Puggaardsgade, one of the curved streets, with houses from the sixteenth to the nineteenth centuries fronting onto the paved street with old-style lamps and protecting stones. ©*Jakob Kieffer-Olsen*

the process is well managed. Provisions for historical research and building surveys are, however, poor.

Archaeological investigations of buildings include dendrochronological dating of removed timber, examination of the roof-construction, measuring, photography, registration of original internal walls etc, and survey of historical sources as insurance-protocols. This work is not carried out on all of the locally protected buildings. Investigations carried out on nationally protected buildings are often inadequate with the results kept in national archives, and the knowledge seldom passed on.

The effect of this on the one hand is the loss of historical information and on the other a lack of knowledge which might inform the management of the next modernisation plan. This problem is connected with shortcomings both in the law and the lack of money needed to pay for any necessary work. The Swedes, of course, have taken care of the historical dimension for a long time.

Turning to the dissemination of information about the history of the buildings and the town itself, the impression of being in the past makes it difficult to provide external information. Currently, this only happens at three sites. The first is the boundary ditch of the ninth century town of Ribe which is not located in an area of old houses but in a car park. It is marked by

84

stones. The two others are the sites of the main medieval town gates which were built in the thirteenth century and removed in the nineteenth century. An inscribed stone marks the site of the southern gate of the town, whilst the site of the northern gate is marked with a similar inscribed stone and with paving stones in a different colour. At the moment, further information about the town can only be found in books, pamphlets, and in museum displays. We have chosen not to put signs on the wall of each house telling its own individual history. At night, darkness is allowed to hide the tower of the Cathedral as there are no laser beams to transform the old town into an outdoor exhibition. At least, not yet.

References

1. Jensen, S., *The Vikings of Ribe*, Den antikvariske Samling, 1991.
2. Ibid.
3. Bencard, M., *Ribe through 1000 years*, Bygd, 1978.
4. Nielsen, I., *Middelalderbyen Ribe*, Centrum, 1985.

9

PRESERVATION OF THE BUILT HERITAGE IN RIBE

Erling Sonne

Ribe city and its surrounding landscape display a harmonious interplay. This is mainly due to the fact that the city is situated on small sand banks in a flat, sparsely forested river valley with extensive meadows, bogs and marshes. As a consequence, the city's potential for growth has been limited to the relatively small areas on the sand banks. Ribe became a densely built-up city with a very clear and precise demarcation between itself and the surrounding countryside and landscape; among other things, this was signified by city gates.

Ribe's special position in the landscape and topographical conditions means that the city has limited potential for growth. This, combined with historical parameters, has meant that the city's development occurs in the form of satellite towns which are clearly separated from the historical core of the city by green meadows and wetlands.

This natural foundation still constitutes the basic element of planning. Nevertheless, it is evident that since the 1960s there has been an increasing demand for new areas to be used for business purposes in connection with the historical city centre. This has led to a weakening of the city front in several places due to the erection of poorly adapted buildings, and demarcation of the city, especially towards the south but also at the northern approach road, is now discordant and without structure. This does not reflect a clear position in terms of planning and architecture.

During recent years, the demand for the development of new growth areas has increased continually. However, at the same time, an increased awareness has emerged among local authoritites and the public regarding the necessity to create a balance between the preservation and extension of the historical environment.

In 1963, Ribe County Council adopted a so-called 'Preservation Declaration' for all houses within the city centre (approximately 500) which meant that all external changes and alterations to buildings had to be approved by Ribe's local authorities (see p. 90). This was to ensure the continued use of materials and craftsmanship in accordance with historical traditions.

The general planning tool currently available is the 'Local Authority Plan',[1] which describes the overall objectives and frameworks in terms of policies and planning for the municipality as a whole. One level below the Local Authority Plan are the local plans, which contain more specific guidelines and provisions for smaller geographical areas and specific projects.

As a more active development in relation to the guidelines and policies of the Local Authority Plan, a document called the 'Ribe Urban Plan' was produced in 1999. Among other things, this plan addresses issues regarding preservation and planning, and connects them to specific development and action plans. The Urban Plan is aimed at citizens, politicians and planners. Its objective is to draw attention to the issues and problems that will require resources in terms of planning and finance in the years to come. The issues and problems are addressed from a holistic point of view. On this basis, principles are established for Ribe's development during the decades to come.

This Urban Plan has the following main themes: Retail Structure, Traffic Structure, Preservation and Urban Renewal, Streets and Squares, Parks and Avenues and City Demarcation. Its main objectives are:

- to secure the historical and cultural environment of Ribe city
- to enhance development of Ribe city as an active and contemporary centre of trade, business, tourism and leisure
- to reduce traffic in the city centre with a view to protecting the urban environment and old houses
- to preserve and improve the well-defined city demarcation against the surrounding wetlands
- to ensure that the development and preservation of Ribe is carried out with a view to creating quality and a good urban environment, through the continuation of its historical traditions.

Even though the plan contains several main areas, the greatest issues of conflict concern the narrow and compact medieval urban structure, and its inability to absorb the ever-increasing traffic, especially during summer. There is a clear conflict of interests between the different roles of Ribe as a residential area, commercial centre, tourist attraction and historical centre; a conflict which can only be resolved by weighing individual interests in relation to the established objectives.

As an example of an overall planning tool, the National Forest and Nature Agency (the government agency responsible for building preservation matters) has prepared so-called 'Preservational Atlases',[2] in conjunction with Danish local authorities. A methodology known as *InterSAVE* is used.[3] The initial drive for the development of this system was the signing of the Granada Convention in 1986.

A Preservation Atlas was developed for Ribe in 1990. It describes the special historical and topographical conditions that have caused the building patterns of Ribe to become so distinctive and special. The Preservation Atlas also indicates the characteristics of individual periods, and indirectly indicates the urban and building elements that can be developed further in terms of quality. The Ribe atlas provides a 'modern' way of combining the traditional view of preservation, which concentrates on individual buildings, with a progressive planning view. It is a more holistic approach to the management of the urban environment.

As a natural consequence of the strategy for preservation work in central Ribe, a series of principles regarding urban design have been developed in order to ensure quality in both preservation and development.

These management tools are mainly used for the renovation of individual houses, display signs, lighting and shop facades, erection of new buildings in historic environments, city parks, avenues, areas within blocks, and last but by no means least, public sector design.

During recent years, a great deal of consideration has been given to the principles to be applied to the development of new buildings. When opportunities are provided for the erection of new buildings – either as individual houses or as inter-connected larger structures – the Local Authority Plan incorporates guidelines for the overall building structures and more detailed provisions providing frameworks for their size and adaptation into the neighbourhood in terms of scale.

Balancing the relative importance of the more detailed and specific principles for building design and materials is a very complex issue and cannot be described in unambiguous terms. The extreme ends of the scale range from constructing buildings which stand out prominently from the existing buildings in terms of design and materials, thus signalling a different era, to building exact replicas of old houses, making it impossible to distinguish between old and new.

In Ribe, the traditional architectural expressions, in terms of design and materials, are being reflected in new design, approaches and modes with a view to having houses appear as individual, independent town houses. An example of this would be the new holiday accommodation – Ribe Holiday Town – comprising 96 flats constructed in such a manner as to constitute a new, clear demarcation of the city centre towards the south. The actual construction plan of Ribe Holiday Town is structurally identical to the plan and layout of the buildings at the old city harbour, and the recurring architectural theme – the gable houses – hail from Ribe's old seventeenth-century gable houses. Nevertheless, the proportions of the houses, their positioning and their distinctive use of traditional tiles and bricks, clearly signal that these buildings were erected in the 1990s.

The use of design briefs faces a series of general problems as technological developments mean that a number of new products and techniques look like old materials, but are easier to work with, cheaper, and are often easier to maintain.

The use of design and development briefs in connection with public spaces is an important and vital factor in the preservation of the historic environment.

During recent decades, the majority of the city streets have been changed from asphalt paving to the original granite paving in accordance with a plan that maps out the historical street system. In addition to this renovation and restoration of the original paving, new squares continue to be established on the basis of historical features regarding scale and materials, thus continuing the development of the historical traditions of Ribe.

The strategy forming the basis for preservation in Ribe takes two sets of planning strategies as its point of departure. One set of planning strategies takes the form of a series of plans registering and appraising houses and environments worth preserving, as well as a series of physical restraints through formal protection (listing) of individual houses. These elements can be described as defensive management tools in relation to preservation values. The other set is more active with the objective of initiating and promoting the rebuilding and improvement of historic environments.

The 1963 Preservation Declaration registered all houses within the city centre[4]. This means that the local authority can require that the external appearance of a building be preserved, and that any changes must have their agreement.

The Ribe Preservation Atlas is a registration document which maps those buildings and environments regarded as being 'worthy of preservation'. However, due to the fact that the Atlas is also capable of contrasting and comparing strengths and weaknesses, it also contributes to the debate on quality in preservation.

In terms of planning, the atlas can constitute an argument – also in political terms – for beginning development of our contemporary history on the basis of familiar elements, yet seen from a new perspective.

The instruments for the actual strategies are more forward-looking and 'active' plans. As an extension of the work of the Preservation Atlas, an 'Urban Renewal Plan' has been prepared for Ribe city, which partly analyses the urban-renewal requirements of individual quarters, and partly presents a plan for future work. The criteria addressed in the Urban Renewal Plan include the constructional standard of floor areas, sanitary/plumbing conditions of dwellings, and the nature and size of open areas within blocks.

The Ribe Preservation Atlas also developed into another active strategy, in so far as it provided the basis for setting up a steering group consisting of business people from outside Ribe and selected civil servants from the local authority of Ribe. This steering group developed a series of objectives for a new urban concept for Ribe, and three working groups prepared proposals for the development of the city and its commerce, while taking into account the desire to preserve, and possibly enhance, the qualities of the city.

A series of projects carried out in Ribe during recent years were based on these reports. Thus, the concept and method have been successful, which is largely due to the special composition of both the steering group and the working group.

The most recent plan to draw attention to an active strategy for preservation work is the previously mentioned Ribe Urban Plan, which addresses current preservation issues in detail and identifies/formulates the areas which require attention.

If sustainable development of historical environments is defined as development which creates new, modern historical layers without compromising the future, then a good basis has been created for the upkeep and preservation of historic towns and cities. It is important to realise that historic towns and cities were created throughout a thousand-year period, where developments have occurred in very small steps. With the technology and knowledge available today, it is possible to change and destroy irreplaceable values within a few years, if we do not display continual awareness, and assess the consequences of our actions in a historical context. That is not to say that change should be prevented, or that everything should be caught in a historical freeze-frame. Quite the opposite, it is a question of managing the change; history is a chain of changes; new things arise and old things disappear – indeed, this is why the old city centre of Ribe is situated on a cultural layer which is three metres deep.

At present, there are no useful tools available which can help local authorities to create new developments with a historical basis. We, consequently, often find that changes are made randomly and lack quality, consistency, coherence and sustainability.

A comparison of the most important historic cities in Denmark reveals a considerable difference in the level and quality of preservation work, and also in the interpretation of the term 'sustainability'. In Ribe we have given great thought to sustainability in the development and preservation projects that we have carried out. Each project has been assessed and adapted so that it will complement the historical context and the city itself.

Change in itself does not present a danger but the rate and frequency of change does. Too many changes too quickly may upset historical continuity.

The trend has been for those tools of preservation and planning used by us in the spirit of preservation, to take the shape of static plans and registrations. They do indeed constitute important bases for preservation, but also reflect a fear of creating new history ourselves.

References

1. Ribe Municipality, *Local Authority Plan for Ribe 1998–2009*, 1998.
2. Ministry of Environment, *Preservational Atlas Ribe*, 1990.
3. Ministry of Environment and Energy/National Forest and Nature Agency, *InterSAVE, International Survey of Architectural Values*, 1995.
4. Ribe City Council, *Declaration of preservation of 16 April 1963 of 550 properties in the inner city*, 1963.

Further Reading

Bencard, M., *Ribe over the last 100 years*, 1978.

Engquist, H.H., *Preservation Plan for Ribe*, 1969.

Ministry of Housing and Building/National Building and Housing Agency, *Urban Renewal and Housing Improvement in Denmark*, 1992.

Planning enterprise Erik Agergård, *Retail Sales in Ribe 1995–2000*, 1995.

Ribe Municipality, *Good Advice on Old Houses*, 1997.

The Craft's Urban-renewal Enterprise, *Urban renewal study in Ribe*, 1991.

University of Southern Denmark, *Regional research: Memorandum 23/91 Tourism in Ribe*, 1991.

10

INTERPRETING HADRIAN'S WALL ON TYNESIDE
Communicating and Celebrating the Near Invisible

Colin Haylock and David Heslop

Although at its extreme the Roman Empire extended considerably further North, with modest remains marking the line of the Antonine Wall, the World Heritage Site of Hadrian's Wall Military Zone represents the most substantive survival of the extreme north-west extent of the Roman Empire.

The Hadrian's Wall Site is in many ways the most complex of the United Kingdom's fifteen World Heritage Sites.

Hadrian's Wall was built around AD 122 and was eventually abandoned in the early fifth century AD. It was originally a complex and sophisticated defensive system which stretched across Britain from the North Sea to the Irish Sea: a continuous structure of varying design running for 117 km, with outlying forts and supply bases extending its influence and control.

After several years in preparation and consultation, a formal Management Plan for the World Heritage Site was published in 1996. This was the first Management Plan prepared for a site in the United Kingdom (UK) and, in terms of process, has formed the model for subsequent work on other UK sites. A key element of the Management Plan was its approach to the distinctive challenges presented by the competing needs of safeguarding and interpreting the Wall as a totality, and in its widely differing component environments. Five years on, the Plan is now undergoing its first formal review.

This paper particularly concentrates on issues of representation and interpretation in the contemporary urban area of Tyneside. This is an area which, with few known and even fewer visible remains of the Wall and associated works, was not originally formally designated as part of the World Heritage Site. Here, the prime challenge has been to develop approaches which achieve the successful interpretation, presentation and celebration of the near invisible.

The conventional and popular conception of Hadrian's Wall is drawn from images of its upstanding remains striding across the open Northumbrian and Cumbrian uplands, images which present a magnificent inter-relationship between landscape and large scale historic human intervention in a relatively hostile environment, a vast distance from the heart of the Roman Empire and the 'civilised world'.

In the upland areas the line of the Wall is generally clearly visible in its remains (Figure 1). Where the line passes through the subsequently established urban areas of Carlisle and Tyneside, upstanding remains become rare. However, in some places the line is still clearly readable, having been retained in the alignment of major roads such as the long and straight West Road and Westgate Road (entry into Newcastle from the west).

Features like this provide a limited contemporary indication of the full extent of the Wall and its related ditch, Military Way and *Vallum,* as a continuous defensive system stretching from coast to coast, a system which at its east end, originally terminated at *Pons Aelius* (Newcastle) and was then extended to *Segedunum* (Wallsend) and supported by an outlying fort and supply base at *Arbeia* (South Shields).

Much of the line and many of the forts and other features have, however, been overlain by many generations of later development which has been unconscious of the underlying archaeology (Figure 2). The areas which now overlie the Wall are generally not traditional archaeological landscapes, and most of them cannot possibly be described as 'sensitive settings'.

Working in this context has presented some interesting problems and opportunities. The key features have been:

- the importance of enabling a contemporary appreciation of the continuity of the original system
- and exploiting the much less sensitive settings in order to undertake forms of interpretation, including representational replication, which greatly help popular understanding but which would be completely inappropriate to the highly sensitive upland settings, and, by diversion, significantly reduce the pressure on these highly sensitive locations with benefits to both the upland and urban areas.

In undertaking work on the largely invisible urban sections of the Wall those involved have had to squarely confront some popular myths concerning the built up areas. Firstly… 'the Wall doesn't exist in the built-up areas' and secondly,… 'because it survives less well, the Wall is less interesting or important in the built-up areas', as well as some professional views that we have nothing more to learn about the Wall in these areas in an archaeological sense.

Excavation in February 2001 in the Shields Road area of Byker, Newcastle, between *Pons Aelius* and *Segedunum,* has provided ample demonstration of

Figure 1B Hadrian's Wall (upper right) on the western outskirts of Newcastle.

Figure 1A Hadrian's Wall in the uplands.

95

Figure 2 Aerial photograph of central Newcastle showing the line of Hadrian's Wall.

Figure 3 Aerial photograph of Shields Road excavation. ©*Airfotos*

the weakness of these myths. William Stukeley's 1725 engraving of Byker shows evidence of the Wall in the area, and Simpson's work in 1928 demonstrated the existence and alignment of the Wall slightly further east in the Fossway area. In the Shields Road area we were, however, dealing with a 'presumed alignment' and the absence of any knowledge of the detailed design of the defensive system and associated works in this area.

The recent excavations have proved extremely rewarding as they show far more than the existence and alignment of the Wall (Figure 3). Of particular importance was the discovery of extensive defensive 'entanglements' in the area forward of the Wall. This has prompted considerable re-thinking of both the role of the Wall – from being a largely symbolic structure to a very real line of defence – and of border conditions at the later stages of Roman regional presence.

In addition to confronting popular myths we have had to address issues of perception related to the value attached to 'Cultural History' in some of the region's most disadvantaged areas. However, the enthusiasm of local politicians and residents for the importance of heritage in the city has been reflected in policies, and the bidding for project programmes such as that now operating under the sixth and final round of the Government's Single Regeneration Budget.

This response has been helped greatly by:

- the dramatic increase in the profile of the Wall as a World Heritage Site, and the importance of the urban sections within this, which has flowed from the nationally and internationally prominent work on the Management Plan, and
- the dramatic exploitation of the interpretation opportunities offered by the urban environment. Exploitation which can be seen at its most substantial in the replication work at Buddle Street in Wallsend, at *Arbeia* Fort in South Shields and now in the recently opened major interpretative facilities at *Segedunum* (Wallsend).

These archaeolgically contentious replications are proving highly effective in their aims of interpreting and exciting. They have clearly stimulated enthusiasm for the more subtle long term work of joining up, marking, interpreting and celebrating the fragments which link these areas to the remainder of the defensive system (Figure 4).

If *Segedunum* and Buddle Street are places where the Wall is visible and well displayed, what are we working with in terms of visible evidence and interpretation elsewhere along the alignment through the urban area of Tyneside?

Figure 4 Buddle Road replication.

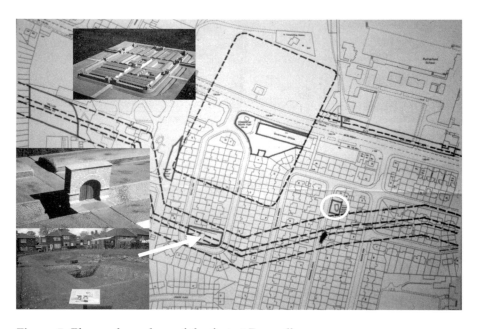

Figure 5 Plan and overlays of the fort at Benwell.

A critical following of the known and presumed alignment reveals a wide range of characters of evidence. Places where the line of the Wall is:

- visible, to those who know what they are looking for, but not interpreted, such as at Denton where the line of the *Vallum* is in a residential open space or the small upstanding remains between a garage forecourt
- visible and well displayed, but in configuration and location not well related to the wider whole – as beside the West Road again at Denton and at *Condercum* Fort and the Temple of *Antenociticus*, both 'lost' in suburban housing in Benwell (Figure 5)
- evident only in the alignment of the modern street system – particularly the dramatic straightness of Fossway and the hilly West and Westgate Roads
- and, possibly most challengingly, partly visible but greatly confused by important and very much more prominent later archaeology, in locations at The Castle Garth in Newcastle and the former Swan Hunter shipyard at Wallsend.

Past well-intentioned approaches have left us with a pattern of interpretation which is equally patchy and varied. As inherited components in the presentation of what has now become part of the World Heritage Site, some of these are of 'delightful domesticity'. Possibly the most extreme of these are:

- the subtle depiction of the Wall profile in the gable of a house, reinforced by a cobbled surface representing the line which has been logically commandeered as a car parking space by the resident; and
- the overwhelmingly railed and gated enclosure at *Condercum* Fort of the only visible *Vallum* crossing anywhere on the Wall, with its sign indicating arrangements for access through a key holder in one of the surrounding suburban houses (Figure 6).

The preparation of the Management Plan for the World Heritage Site allowed everyone with involvement and interests in issues relating to the Wall to stand back from and rise above the current problems and deficiencies related to its urban sections and to recognise their importance to the totality of the system and to begin to develop and apply strategies for addressing them.

Work on the Tyneside urban section brought together English Heritage, the three Local Authorities, the then Countryside Commission, the members of the Hadrian's Wall Tourism Partnership, Tyne and Wear Museums and the local universities. This group worked on and developed further the

Figure 6 Fencing at Condercum.

Figure 7 CityLife.

Management Plan's principal recommendations for the urban sections which were to:

- improve the protection of remains
- increase the visibility of remains
- increase the linkage between individual elements
- re-establish the linear character of the system
- and encourage research of the course and history of the operation of the frontier system.

A key element in this group's work was the joint commissioning and management of a Local Interpretative Plan for Hadrian's Wall on Tyneside. This was prepared by PLB Design Ltd with Transport For Leisure (TFL) and reported in June 1998.

In summary the report stressed the need to be innovative and creative in promoting and popularising the archaeology of the Wall in this area, and the need for a co-ordinated strategy for this and its delivery which embraced all the key partners and stakeholders. In practical terms it made recommendations for an action plan to be co-ordinated by English Heritage which would:

- increase awareness of the World Heritage Site
- promote better local understanding
- emphasise the benefit of investment in heritage.

In addition it provided practical advice in the areas of:

- identity and branding
- signage and display
- the development of individual sites
- sources of public and private finance to help realise the proposals.

The report was adopted by all of the joint commissioning bodies. Its core recommendations are now being carried through with the help of Government Single Regeneration Budget (SRB), financial assistance. This funding helps to support an interpretation strategy which is focused upon:

- developing infrastructure
- investing in 'museum' facilities
- developing new gateway facilities for economic tourism.

and includes specific programmes aimed at raising awareness of the Wall visually through 'Marking the Wall', and in literature through 'Writing on the Wall'.

Through the patterns of thinking generated by the Management Plan and the Local Interpretative Plan, the Wall and the traces of Roman life 'beneath our feet' on Tyneside are featuring more and more frequently in contemporary educational and cultural activity (Figure 7). Examples of this have ranged from re-enactments to exploration, and re-interpretation in exhibition art such as some elements of the VANE 2000 programme of 80 temporary exhibitions in Newcastle in October and November 2000.

Increasingly Hadrian's Wall on Tyneside is being recognised as an integral and valuable part of the region's premier heritage asset. Appreciation is growing, underscored by the new facilities at Segedunum, that 'The Wall Begins Here!'. This represents a strong start to changing perceptions. The endeavour, however, still has a long way to go to achieve the core objectives for the urban sections themselves and for their contribution to the interpretation and management of visitor pressure on the Wall as a whole. To help achieve this the Wall on Tyneside still needs:

- the development of orientation and gateway facilities for people arriving in the region by various forms of transport
- a high quality marketing campaign
- better branding and information
- an even stronger programme of innovative events and arts initiatives
- and still better definition and reinforcement of the linearity and continuous nature of the original system.

The Management Plan refers to the change in perceptions of the importance of the Wall in the rural areas, from a time when 30 years before there had been two active quarries on the line of the Wall. In the urban areas similar changes in perception have made dramatic advances in the past five years. The current review of the Management Plan and the implementation of the SRB programme and subsequent activity should allow similarly thought provoking comparisons in another 25 years, this time about the treatment and significance of the Wall in the urban areas. To achieve this we will have had to have been successful in securing, through the expanding range of methods becoming available to us, our original objective in interpreting Hadrian's Wall on Tyneside – that of 'communicating and celebrating the near invisible'.

11

CHANGING LANDSCAPES
Prehistory in the Danish Countryside

Ulf Näsman, in collaboration with
Charlotte Fabech and Jytte Ringtved

In the nineteenth century, Denmark made a significant contribution to the development of archaeology. Due to the political and intellectual movements of the century, the prehistoric past and its visible monuments became important elements in the construction of a new Danish identity, especially after the defeat of the Prussians in 1864. Today, prehistoric monuments are still a well-known element in the landscape, and an appreciated part of Danish cultural heritage. In fact, some sites and monuments rank among our national symbols.

There is, therefore, no problem in advocating that the presence of archaeological remains in the landscape is a resource worthy of protection and care. Scheduled monuments are well protected in Denmark. At the same time, however, most users of the landscape, including planners and administrators, have great difficulties in understanding the real character of the archaeological heritage, *i.e.* that most of it is both invisible and unknown. For too long, the authorities, including the archaeological, have demonstrated a surprising lack of understanding of how great and varied the threats are against the buried cultural heritage. It has only recently been realised that little of what is preserved is in fact protected effectively.[1]

Danish archaeology has followed a defensive strategy for too long. It is a strategy dominated by rescue excavations rather than by recording and *in situ* preservation. The focus is on excavations, and on the splendid objects which are occasionally found and presented to the public in the media and in exhibitions. The focus on excavations and finds has given the public the impression that a large part of the archaeological heritage has already been excavated – 'Is there still something to find?' – and that the heritage is in good hands in our museum stores. This perhaps reflects the lack of interest in theoretical issues which characterised Danish archaeology of the late 1980s and 1990s.[2]

It is often argued that more money given to rescue work would solve the problem. There is no doubt that rescue archaeology in Denmark lacks both resources and proper organisation, but it is unrealistic to try and save the archaeological heritage through excavation alone. For instance, few settlements, one of the most important archaeological sources, are protected. The remaining thousands of sites, which in reality are without any protection, are destroyed at a rate with which hundreds of excavations could not keep up. I assume that the situation is similar in most European countries.

Nevertheless, Danish archaeology can be proud of its long tradition of recording and preservation. A record of visible monuments and sites has been kept and updated since the nineteenth century.[3] After the defeat of the Prussians, it was possible for the curators of the National Museum to persuade the government to take an initiative to register ancient monuments. The nationalistic feelings made the construction of a glorious national history an important task. Naturally, the early record of the archaeological content in the landscape consisted almost entirely of visible monuments, which meant more or less well preserved ancient monuments.

Few excavations took place in the nineteenth century, nor was field walking carried out or any other forms of reconnaissance used. The national record of sites and monuments was improved throughout the last century, and today includes many invisible but identified sites as well as sites that have been destroyed. But proper use of the record must be based on an understanding of what it in fact represents.

The main purpose of the record was and still is to serve archaeological rescue work and to some extent landscape planning as well. The record has also been used to produce distribution maps with the intention of presenting prehistoric reality, one way or the other. It has to be realised, however, that recorded monuments represent nothing but detached elements of vanished landscapes. For instance, a map of Neolithic monuments and sites will primarily be a map of the present, showing our knowledge of megalithic graves in the landscape today. In relation to the Neolithic landscape, the record is nothing but disconnected dots on a map. Most traces of the prehistoric landscapes are hidden below the surface and unrecorded. The record represents a more or less random pattern of visible peaks in this buried landscape.

The present rural landscape is the result of late eighteenth and early nineteenth-century land reforms, as well as the rapidly changing methods of cultivation in the twentieth century. The majority of the once large areas of meadow, pasture, open forest and heath became cultivated as a result of the re-distribution of land holdings. The old landscape that disappeared was in its turn the result of continuous land-use since at least the middle of the first millennium AD and formed particularly during the Middle Ages. When the archaeological record was started in the nineteenth century, remains of the old landscape were still present in many areas where land reforms had not yet completely altered the rural structure. It was not acknowledged then, however, that the meadows, pastures, moors, and open forests, which constitute the landscape surrounding the ancient monuments, were part of the same landscape history, and were, therefore, as important as the graves and mounds themselves. Nor was it realised that this landscape reflected the same society that had left the ancient mounds preserved until then. Consequently, the landscape around the monuments has lacked protection, and in most cases has been completely changed by modern land-use.

Today, minute areas representing traditional land-use remain in the agrarian-industrial landscape and they have only been preserved with difficulty, and primarily as nature reserves. For instance, only 3% of modern Denmark is covered by meadows whereas in c.1800 it was 25%.[4] Nothing is left of the once characteristic forest pastures. We have to go to southern Sweden to find nature reserves of this type. The main argument of landscape managers for the protection of the so-called semi-cultural nature (heaths, meadows, permanent pastures) is, unfortunately, not their value as historic remains but their present ecological value and their contribution to the preservation of bio-diversity. Consequently, the methods used to preserve them is often not based on an understanding of historic land-use but on biological arguments.

To a certain extent, the first record of sites and monuments became a record of the picturesque rather than the usual and commonplace. This is revealed by the representation of ancient monuments in contemporary pictorial art. Indeed, ancient monuments became a popular motif of nineteenth century landscape painting. The nineteenth-century artist depicted a dolmen beautifully situated in a pasture surrounded by grazing cattle whereas a twentieth-century photographer will only find the scheduled Neolithic grave preserved. It will be situated in the middle of a deep-ploughed grain field in a predominantly urbanised landscape, without public access. In this way, the visible ancient monuments have become detached from their landscape setting.

The visual appearance of ancient monuments in the modern countryside strengthens the misapprehension that ancient monuments are leftovers from ancient times and, therefore, have no connection to the modern landscape. This attitude characterises Danish archaeological work in the landscape, to a certain extent, whereby protected ancient monuments are taken care of as isolated spots in the landscape. Sometimes the visible monuments are supplemented by knowledge about the invisible prehistoric remains, but we normally know too little about the buried archaeology to be able to use it. This deplorable situation is not unique to Denmark.

Landscape archaeologists study the original landscape context of an excavated site, but its transformation into the present is rarely discussed in Denmark. The normal approach is synchronic, i.e. ancient monuments are looked upon as remains of that past reality of which they once formed an integral part. Thus, they are studied in chronological isolation, with no relation to the later historic contexts in which they have survived. The present context in which they have to survive today is often considered irrelevant. In contrast, the strong impact of historical geography has influenced the perspective of landscape archaeology in Sweden. The spatial relationship between the ancient monuments and the landscape has consequently received greater attention and studies are of course diachronic. Swedish archaeologists also reflect on the use of ancient monuments by later generations.[5] Ancient monuments, therefore, function both as historic representations of past landscapes and as contemporary elements integrated into today's landscape.

- The approach of Danish landscape management is characterised by an ideological divide between culture and nature.
- Isolated protected monuments and sites dominate the perspective of archaeologists and museum curators. The focus is on past landscapes so the present landscape is, therefore, seen as irrelevant.
- The ideal of a virgin nature without human impact fills the perspective of the biologists. Left to 'free dynamics', a landscape will turn back to its 'natural' condition so landscape history is irrelevant.

Both parties neglect the reality. One party does not consider the fact that all Danish landscapes over the millennia have been created and re-shaped in an intimate interaction between man and nature. Virgin nature is a myth. The other party does not understand that archaeological remains are not only constituents of past landscapes but they also have value because they exist here and now, as elements of today's landscape.

This means that the perspective of landscape history on the one hand and the perspective of nature on the other are not integrated in landscape planning today. Nor is the holistic view that the landscape is seen as a biocultural product sufficiently implemented.[6] The situation is made worse by a serious imbalance between culture and nature in Danish landscape management. The biological competence is largely at county level (the regional planning body) but the archaeological and historical competence is almost absent there. It is to be found in the museums, which are, however, neither strong nor well integrated in the planning process. The result is a fragmented administration of the landscape in which the archaeological and historical heritage is forgotten and frequently neglected.

Fortunately, the Danish ministry of the environment has recently recommended that the cultural heritage in the landscape should be given more attention. Following the general trend in European landscape management, it is emphasised that the administration must not only care for the single monument or site, but has to look at the larger entireties of culture heritage and their contexts. We can now look forward to the development of a better and integrated administration of the landscape.

The ancient monuments and sites should be looked upon as constituents of a 'cultural landscape' in the same way that wild plants and animals are seen as part of the 'natural surrounding'. Our stock of historic remains is threatened by population decline and extermination. It is a situation which is similar in many ways to that of rare plants and animals. In fact, ancient monuments and sites can be considered to be at greater risk since they cannot reproduce themselves.

It is important to realise that the preserved and visible monuments are only a distorted representation of the past in the present, left by the past as a societal construction. Some sites were left for religious reasons and were protected for a long time by religious beliefs and rituals. Grave monuments are the largest group among these sites. They are now protected by legislation. Other sites became obsolete and were either left to themselves or forgotten about in uncultivated areas. They were only preserved because later land-use did not destroy them. This is a rare type represented by, for example, the few preserved field systems of the early Iron Age. The largest part of the archaeological heritage is, however, to be found in areas suitable for cultivation, and we can expect to find them in arable land. The buried sites are, therefore, usually both unknown and unprotected.

If we wish the visible archaeological monuments to be more than decoration in a postcard landscape, we also have to consider the buried heritage which is the largest number of archaeological sites. Our main problem today is not the protection and care of the scheduled ancient monuments and sites, but the unintentional wearing down of the historic content of the landscape.

It is the continuous history and entirety of the landscape which is the starting-point of the study of landscape history today. This perspective should also constitute the basis of the administration of the archaeological heritage in the landscape. The everyday landscape is the result of historical changes throughout the millennia. Traces of earlier land-use can be seen or found everywhere: ancient monuments, buildings, borders, the settlement pattern, the location of arable land, meadows, pastures, moors, forests poor and fertile soils, etc. Some periods are well represented with visible monuments which are well-known elements in the familiar Danish landscape. These periods are, consequently, well-represented in the new county schedules of historic heritage sites. Other periods are represented by invisible remains and are thus available only as elements of a landscape history, provided that the story is told. Of course, these periods are largely forgotten in the new listing of the historical heritage.

Landscape management underestimates the value of the invisible or hardly visible archaeological heritage, and the archaeological authorities have overlooked the major threats for too long. Recent initiatives will, hopefully, improve the situation[8], but we believe that proper planning tools are absent in the Danish administration, since the national record of sites and monuments cannot give us a realistic representation of the buried heritage.

At present, little is done to protect the invisible heritage. The focus of the revised Museum Act has been to improve the conditions of the rescue work but not the protection and preservation of the archaeological heritage. The main threat is not only the daily wear and tear of agriculture but also that the constructions made in connection with infrastructure and urbanisation are destructive. The invisibility of the largest part of the archaeological heritage – and the most valuable part, in my opinion – is the main administrative problem. How can you visualise the invisible?

In historical landscape research projects, it is common to make tentative reconstructions of past landscapes based on present knowledge about settlement patterns and land-use in different periods. A relatively precise knowledge enables fairly detailed reconstructions of the fourteenth century settlement pattern and the surrounding landscape with arable, meadows, pasture, wood pasture, wilderness, etc.[9] It is possible to present hypothetical, but still fairly reliable, maps of the landscape in c. AD 1000, based on archaeology and a retrogressive use of later sources. In the Merovingian period, the sources are already so few that the limited number of recorded settlements makes all attempts to reconstruct settlement pattern and land-use, using traditional archaeological methods, uncertain.

The methods used for making these kind of reconstructed maps are time consuming and aimed at research. Museum curators and landscape administrators should be given a better tool for appreciating the archaeological potential of a given area, one based on modern GIS-analysis. In the research centre 'Changing Landscapes', it has been one of our aims to try to develop methods that can produce indicative models of prehistoric land-use and settlement pattern.[10] The basis for our work is easily accessible records, primarily the national record of sites and monuments.

In his Ph.D. thesis, Bo Ejstrud has used statistical methods to produce indicative maps of the plausible occurrence of sites from the Mesolithic, Neolithic, Bronze Age and early Iron Age.[11] The data set is the relationship between archaeological finds and soil types, sloping terrain, proximity to running water and lakes, etc., and the results seem to be interesting for research as well as a promising tool to support archaeologists in landscape planning.

Based on a richer source material, Charlotte Fabech and Jytte Ringtved have produced the preliminary results about the landscape from the late Roman period to the Viking Age. One of our laboratory areas is situated at Bjerringbro to the northwest of Århus in east Jutland. Space only allows a few maps to be presented.[12]

The few finds from the third to eleventh centuries make it difficult to evaluate the relationship between the settlement of this period and the traditional land-use as recorded c. 1800 (Figure 1). As a first step to improving our chances of getting an impression of the early forest cover, Charlotte Fabech and Jytte Ringtved have supplemented the forests and groves that we find on the earliest maps (c. 1800) with the locations of all place-names which indicate forest and areas characterised by steep slopes or heavy clay. Regardless of their possible date, they are simply used to indicate where wood could have been standing during the last 1000 years or so (Figure 2).

Place-names characteristic of the period from the third to the eighth centuries can be used to get an idea of which areas were settled in these centuries. Name-types also familiar in those parts of England where Danes settled (primarily ending in -by or –thorp) were certainly found in the Viking Age. In our opinion they represent a settlement shuffle and expansion in the period from the late Merovingian eighth century to the High Middle Ages. A later series of names can be interpreted as a result of a continued settlement expansion in the High Middle Ages. Carefully used, place-names can enable an understanding of the settlement development in the area.

Present parish churches are often Romanesque, dating to the twelfth century, but it is likely that several of them had wooden predecessors dating back to the late Viking Age. A number of excavations have demonstrated that we can expect to find a late Viking Age settlement close to many Romanesque churches. This is probably due to the fact that Viking Age magnates paid for the erection of most of the early churches. Romanesque churches may indicate that an area was settled in the Viking Age.

Numerous rescue excavations show that Viking Age settlements as well as those from the late Roman, Migration, or Merovingian periods are usually found a few hundred metres from a historic hamlet or village.[13] This is important because it clearly indicates that the intensively used areas of the High Medieval landscape were more or less continuously used from the second century AD.

This is confirmed by another study carried out in collaboration with the Danish Institute of Agricultural Sciences. In 1844 each field in the area had its soil classified according to a scale from zero (worst) to 24 (best). High soil classifications are found close to the historical hamlets and villages, which mostly date back to the High Middle Ages, and the relation is especially clear for those with names of an early type and thus a continuous manuring of the infield. It is also an important observation that nearly all archaeological finds from the second half of the first millennium are associated with good soils. In fact, good soil seems to be a gigantic archaeological monument for farming history. An important conclusion of the soil studies is that the presence of good soils is an indicator for settlements from the period between

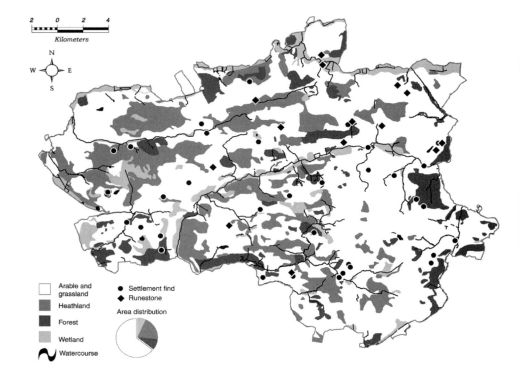

Figure 1 The research area around Bjerringbro, east Jylland, consists of 32 parishes. Here land-use is based upon a map of c. 1800, and we see the arable land and pasture/dry meadow (white), heath (mid-grey), forests and groves (dark grey), and wetland (light grey). Finds from the late Roman period to the Viking Age are marked with round dots and runestones with a diamond. Note that very few finds are found in the heaths.

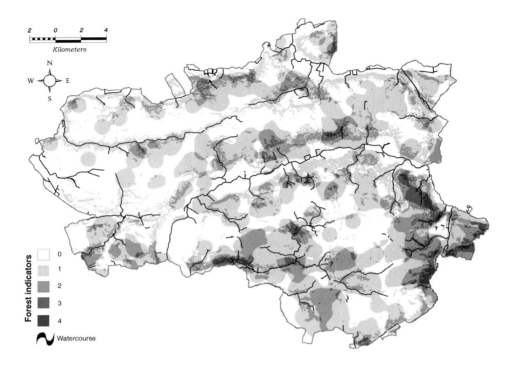

Figure 2   A map showing the probability that an area was covered by forest in the first and second millennia. It is based on records of early forest cover, on place-names indicating forest, and on areas with steep slopes or heavy clay. It is clear that the eastern part probably had the densest tree cover.

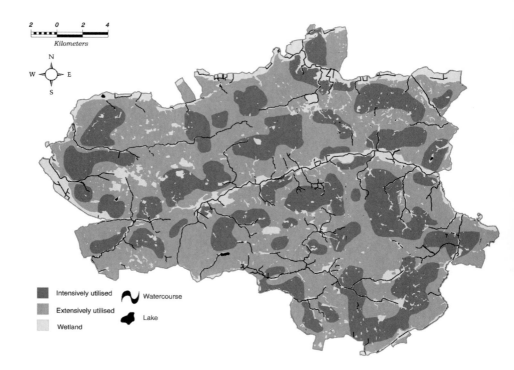

Figure 3   A map indicating which areas were intensively used and settled (white) and those that were intensively used (dark grey) from the late Roman period to the Viking Age. It is based on archaeological records, historic maps, place-names, soil classifications, etc.

the Late Roman third century and the late Viking Age eleventh century in the same area.

The preliminary result is a map which indicates the areas that were intensively used and settled and those which were extensively used in the period (Figure 3). We do not of course state that archaeological finds are lacking in the extensively used areas, but assume that the number of finds in these areas is much lower than in those intensively used. Bo Ejstrud's work has demonstrated that finds may be more plentiful in other periods. For example we expect – and know – that Mesolithic finds are to be found along the wetland areas.

If we wish buried archaeological interests to be seriously considered when the future landscape is planned, it is necessary, in our opinion, to develop planning tools, which can be used at a level comparable to the way regional planning is used for agriculture, industry, infrastructure, nature, tourism, water resources, etc. Such a tool must be spatial, and cannot be based on dots as in present rescue work. The national record of sites and monuments is still, of course, the first map layer in any archaeological landscape characterisation. Maps indicating the possible occurrence of buried sites from each relevant historical landscape period are the next layers. In 'Changing Landscapes' we have demonstrated how indicative maps can be produced. A last layer is an interim map of the antiquarian priorities. In our work we are inspired by England's Historic Landscape Characterisation programme,[14] as well as by work in the Netherlands. Tools have to be developed, however, to fit in with national legislation, the history of the regional landscape, and the organisation of antiquarian work. Our approach is, therefore, an attempt to fit a Danish situation.

In a new project Agrar-2000 we continue our work on historic landscape reconstructions and try to apply it to other landscape types.[15] We hope, of course, that indicative maps will be thoroughly tested in the daily routine of a Danish county as well as at a regional museum.

References

1. Jørgensen, A.N. and Pind, J. (eds), *Før landskabets erindring slukkes, Rapport fra arkæologikonference på Nationalmuseet d. 22–23 marts 2000,* Rigsantikvaren & Det arkæologiske Nævn, 2001.
2. Fabech, C. et al, 'Settlement and Landscape – a presentation of a research programme and a conference', in Fabech, C. and Ringtved, J. (eds), *Settlement and Landscape,* Jutland Archaeological Society, 1999, pp. 13–28.
3. See Henrik Jarl-Hansen's paper in this volume.
4. Larsen, S.N. and Vikstrøm, T., *Ferske enge – en beskyttet naturtype,* Skov- og Naturstyrelsen, Summary, 1995.

5. Zachrisson, T., 'Folkminnen om fornminnen – ett annat landskap', in Antell, E. (ed), *Landskapets andliga dimension*, Riksantikvarieämbetet, Kulturmiljövård, 1994/5, pp. 40–45.
6. Gren, L., 'Surveying the cultural heritage of the Swedish countryside', in *Current Swedish Archaeology* 8, 2000, pp. 51–66.
7. See Jørgensen, A.N. and Pind, J. (eds), *Før landskabets erindring slukkes. Rapport fra arkæologikonference på Nationalmuseet d. 22–23 marts 2000*, Rigsantikvaren & Det arkæologiske Nævn, 2001.
8. See Carsten Paludan Muller's article in this volume.
9. Berglund, B.E. (ed), *The Cultural Landscape During 6000 Years in Southern Sweden – the Ystad Project*, Lund/København Ecological bulletins, 41, 1991.
10. See www.sdu.dk/Hum/ForandLand/English/Index.htm.
11. Ejstrud, B., *At spå om fortiden*, 2001. Only available www.ou.dk/Hum/ForandLand/Dansk/historiskforsk/modelark/forside.htm (6 August 2001).
12. Fabech, C. and Ringtved, J., *Udpegninger af områder med intensiv arealudnyttelse fra ca 150 e.Kr. til 1100 e.K*, 2001. Only available www.ou.dk/Hum/ForandLand/Dansk/Scenarieforsk/arkaearb.htm (3 August 2001).
13. Callmer, J., 'To stay or to move', in *Meddelanden från Lunds universitets historiska museum, New Series* 6, 1985–1986, pp. 167–208.
14. Fairclough, G. (ed), *Historic landscape characterisation*, English Heritage, 1999.
15. See www.natmus.dk/agrar2000/.

Further Reading

Etting, V. (ed), *På opdagelse i kulturlandskabet*, Gyldendal, 1995.
Helmfrid, S. (ed), *Sveriges Nationalatlas. Kulturlandskapet och bebyggelsen*, Bra Böcker, 1994.

12

HISTORIC ENVIRONMENTS OF THE NORTH SEA
Towards an Information System for the Cultural Landscape

Henrik Jarl Hansen

In common with many other parts of the world, there is a long lived tradition in Denmark of collecting old artefacts and recording information about the country's historical and archaeological past. Some of the interest probably has to do with natural human curiosity, perhaps with some added superstition. Where were the giants and the ancient kings buried and where were the golden treasures hidden? Neolithic polished stone axes were regarded as thunderbolts and were used along with belemnites and sea urchins for both personal protection and for the protection of houses and animals. The prehistoric burial mounds were natural elements in the cultural landscape and myths and legends were linked with many of them.

When the systematic recording of the country's archaeological past began in the late nineteenth century, it was still possible to document some of these stories. They are now kept, along with archaeological information about the sites and monuments, at the National Museum in Copenhagen where they are also digitised.[1,2] There are several stories, and at least one of them could be relevant to the theme of this book. In 1876 a local schoolteacher J. Nielsen recorded the many well preserved burial mounds in the Vestervig parish in the north-western part of Jutland, close to the North Sea. Across the parish border to the south-east there is a pronounced hill visible in the landscape. Nielsen wrote: [3]

> It is noted that there is still a legend in the district which says that a
> ship of gold is hidden in the hill, which could pay all of Denmark's

national debt at its time of greatest need. But anybody who digs for it before that time shall die within a year.

The legend could be referring to one of the old kings of the North Sea buried in his ship and ready to set sail. In theory, it may be a parallel to the well-known ship burial from Sutton Hoo, Suffolk, found in 1939.[4] But who dares to excavate and find out if the story is true under these circumstances?

The fact that myths and legends were linked with many of the burial mounds has presumably saved several of them from premature destruction, not least in cases where death and destruction were promised to those who dared to violate the sanctity of the grave. In fact there is a high concentration of preserved prehistoric barrows in the area around Vestervig. The protective role of myths and legends is now taken over by legal protection and the stories connected to the sites are almost forgotten by the locals. However, it is interesting to note that in Iceland today folklore still plays an important part in the country's cultural heritage. Dwellings of the hidden people or elves are still registered in the archaeological field surveys of Iceland and it is often the case that these dwellings in boulders or mounds are shown more respect from the public than man-made archaeological remains.[5]

A NATIONAL ARCHAEOLOGICAL DATABASE

As already mentioned, the systematic recording of the archaeological heritage in Denmark was begun in the late nineteenth century. It was carried out on a national scale, complementing earlier initiatives going as far back as the seventeenth century. In 1807 the present National Museum was founded, after which the collection of information on Danish prehistoric finds and monuments accelerated dramatically. The foundation for our subsequent computerisation is therefore rather unique, as we are able to build upon centuries of systematic collection of archaeological information.

Establishing a national database of archaeological sites and monuments and related information has been the task of The Danish National Record for Culture History (DKC) at the National Museum in Copenhagen since it was instituted by the Museum Act of 1984. In 1997 DKC joined the inter-disciplinary research centre 'Changing Landscapes'.[6] The aim was to create an Information System for the Cultural Landscape using GIS as a tool. The centre has now come to an end and it is time for evaluation. It is also time for visions as a new Museum Act is on its way in Denmark with a demand for the implementation of an efficient planning tool for the cultural landscape and for the protection of the archaeological heritage. The development of such a tool is what we have been working on both within the 'Changing Landscapes' project and in another multi-disciplinary research project: 'Agrar 2000'.[7] The two projects have a number of similarities, focussing as they do on the cultural landscape and with a strong emphasis on strategic aspects. One of the aims has been to develop methods and tools of use for the management of the landscape.

It is a major undertaking to compile a national overview of the country's archaeological heritage, even in a country the size of Denmark (approx 43,100 sq km). This was the case when the so-called parish surveys were begun in 1873, regardless of whether the recording was carried out by walking the moors of Jutland or using a horse-drawn carriage. All sites were systematically recorded, parish by parish, in hand-written reports, and located on survey maps. It is still true today, with the present process of digitising the original descriptions and the maps, and making them accessible in electronic format.

Another of today's duties is the systematic recording of all new finds and archaeological excavations reported by the country's many archaeological museums. This information is demanded by the Museum Act, in order to create a national overview. It amounts to approximately 2,000–3,000 reports each year (Figure 1).

TOWARDS AN INFORMATION SYSTEM FOR THE CULTURAL HERITAGE

The map shown on Figure 1 is made up of the location of the 145,000 archaeological sites which we know exist in Denmark. However, it is more than just a map of the prehistoric settlement. It is also a map which reflects centuries of archaeological activity as well as a map of our present electronic recording of the archaeological knowledge. It can be argued, therefore, that it also shows the mapping of some of the factors mentioned above e.g. construction work and intensive farming. As a result of these activities, it is obvious that most of the recorded sites are no longer visible in the landscape, but they are not necessarily totally destroyed. We still have to take their possible remains into consideration when planning future activities in the landscape. That is why it is so important to develop an efficient and reliable information system for the cultural landscape which can be used by both archaeologists and planners. In order to optimise the system it must be able to handle factual as well as hypothetical information about the location of the sites in the landscape. It is not only a question of which archaeological sites exist in a given area but also an estimate of their extent and what type of sites are still likely to be found.

Most of the locations of the archaeological sites known from the early surveys, and also from later recordings, are only represented on the archaeological maps and in the database as point data. This is sufficient when it comes to the presentation of the cultural heritage on large-scale maps. However, it is not adequate for use in physical planning. Point data has to be

Figure 1 Map of Denmark with the distribution of the 145,000 archaeological sites recorded in the national database.

transformed into areas, so one of the more important issues is to develop methods to transform today's point data into surfaces via analysis of the landscape characteristics, thus providing a more adequate representation of a prehistoric or historic reality.

It is also important to build the knowledge into the system that 'white spots' on archaeological distribution maps do not necessarily mean that there are no cultural-historic remains to be found in the area. They are most likely just a sign of the lack of archaeological activity, which occurs in some countries when the archaeological recording process has not yet been completed.[8]

This kind of predictive data should be supplemented with information about the actual demarcations known from archaeological excavations, surveys or observations. The range of accuracy presented will vary from modern GPS surveys with a precision in three dimensions within a few centimetres, to information based upon old survey maps with an estimated accuracy of less than 25–50 m or maybe even worse in some instances. In most cases it is impossible to check or to improve the information because the archaeological site in question has most likely been destroyed. So the information system must be able to handle and present different levels of accuracy to its users.

THE NATIONAL ARCHAEOLOGICAL DATABASE ON THE INTERNET

In 1997 DKC made the national Sites and Monuments database available on the Internet,[9] primarily as a tool for archaeologists. The site has since then become a popular tool for museum professionals in their daily work, as well as for researchers. The concept behind the site is on-line access to all of the information in the national database combined with the ability to carry out simple queries and to present the result on a range of modern topographical maps in scales from 1:2,000,000 to 1:25,000. Until now full access has only been given to users within a limited range of museum professionals, researchers and students. The public has only had access to maps in scale 1:200,000 and to limited information about the sites. This has essentially been done for two reasons. The first one is economic and related to the copyright of the digitised maps. The second is based upon an ongoing discussion within the archaeological community and a wish to protect sensitive data. In other words, it should not be possible to produce treasure-hunter maps directly from the Internet. On the other hand, there is a growing understanding that it may be better for the public to know about the cultural-historic sites in order to protect them rather than locking the information away. How can you protect something that you do not know exists? Naturally this point of view will vary from country to country depending on size, infrastructure, etc. One should not forget that looting of archaeological sites and the illegal trade in archaeological objects and stolen antiquities is a major problem in many countries and is often closely associated with the international drug trade. However, in a densely populated country like Denmark and with a strong professional presence in the local society, it is a question of how much the damage would be compared to the possible benefits. Professional treasure hunters can always consult the printed literature in order to find out where to go, and there is no doubt that the public in general wants to be able to access the information about the country's cultural history.

In order to improve access to the archaeological information, DKC launched a new version of the national database on the Internet in 2001. Apart from changes in design, the major improvement was access to orthophotos (aerial photos as maps) and to historical maps, both of which are national in coverage. This means that the professional user can see the cultural-historic sites presented on a wide range of modern topographical maps as well as on historical maps and aerial photos. The historical maps available on DKC online are at a scale of 1:20,000, hand-coloured and produced in the late nineteenth century, at a time before the expansion of the cities and before major drainage of the wetland areas took place in order to create more arable land. The use of historical maps as part of the Information System on the Internet gives a new visible dimension to the distribution of the archaeological phenomena, but not yet the power of a professional GIS-system.

This will probably be the case with the next version of DKC on the Internet, which is not far away. The mapping system used has been developed, until now, 'in-house'. In the new system we will probably introduce a commercial GIS-system in order to be able to handle the point-related information as well as areas and surfaces. In the existing system the maps are all presented in raster format. With the use of GIS, it is also possible to present maps and other data in vector format with all the possibilities this means for making distribution maps, predictive modelling, etc. However, we have to bear in mind that it is not enough to concentrate on the technical side of the tool. It is just as important that the data which sits behind it is available and of high quality. This is why it is also important to speed up the ongoing recording process in order to be able to access information of the same quality for the whole of the country and thereby live up to the intentions of the new Museum Act.

As an initiative in connection with the new Act, the Danish Ministry of Culture plans to carry out a national mapping of the most important areas of archaeological interest and to make the information available in electronic form for the planning authorities and for the individual site owners. This is also why it is important to develop a third generation of DKC online with the full functionality of a professional GIS-system. This should make it easier to include the consideration of the archaeological heritage in the development of the future cultural landscape.

ARCHAEOLOGY IN A CHANGING ENVIRONMENT

In 1900 a reference work was published as a result of an inter-disciplinary scientific research project on 'kitchen middens', which are located in large numbers along the Danish coastline.[10] The middens, which are mainly from the Stone Age, consist of deposits of seashells (mainly oysters), animal bones and flint artefacts, up to 2 m thick. It was this type of site, first recorded in 1837, which led to the Danish words *køkkenmødding* (kitchen midden) and *Ertebølle* being added to the international archaeological terminology.

A century later an archaeological conference was held in the spring of 2000 on the future for Danish archaeology in the light of the massive destruction of the cultural-historic remains that has taken place during the past century. Many types of archaeological remains have suffered from recent human activity in the landscape and one of the most damaged site types is the 'kitchen middens'. These sites are often located in areas which are used today for cultivation, gravel-extraction, re-forestation or for recreational purposes. Recent investigations into the state of preservation of the shell middens demonstrate that about 90% of them are now almost gone and that the rest may disappear over the next decade.[11]

Many other types of archaeological remains also suffer severe damage. About 75% of the barrows that were recorded during the first national surveys mentioned above are now gone. However, it is the non-visible archaeological remains like medieval deposits in town centres, prehistoric settlements and graves, which are in the most dramatic situation. In order to prevent, or at least to slow down the process of destruction, it is necessary to protect the archaeological heritage by law. This is apparently not enough. It is also important to record the remains and to make these records available for museum professionals, planners and the public in order to make everybody aware of the fragile archaeological resource.

As already discussed, making this information generally available is a double-edged sword. The information can be used in order to protect and preserve but it can also be misused for looting and destruction. Who creates most damage – the amateur-archaeologist collecting flint artefacts from the field or the farmer ploughing the artefacts to the surface? Like the visible prehistoric remains, non-visible ones can be taken into consideration in the farmer's production plans just like other factors related to modern cultivation. Nowadays farmers also use GPS and computers. In the end it is probably a question of compensation, a topic not unknown to European agricultural society. For that reason, we need reliable and accurate information about the known archaeological remains, their preservation and their presence in the landscape. However, it is not only the physical cultivation that threatens archaeology. Drainage, expansion of cities and the infrastructure play a major role, and we must cover all aspects in order to prevent archaeology in the future from only existing in glossy publications and as virtual reality in national databases and GIS-systems.

CONCLUSIONS

Besides museum professionals and planners, the public has to be involved in the protection of the remaining cultural-historic remains. Stories of death or destruction are no longer sufficient for their protection but they may help the preservation process. If the stories about the sites are forgotten and the sites themselves are kept secret, few will miss them when they are gone. We have to bear this fact in mind when developing our future information systems for the cultural landscape.

References

1.   Christoffersen, J., 'The Danish National Record of Sites and Monuments, DKC', in Larsen, C.U. (ed), *Sites & Monuments. National Archaeological Records,* The National Museum of Denmark, DKC, 1992, pp. 7–22.

2.   Hansen, H.J., 'Archaeology computerised; dream or reality?', in Hansen, H.J. and Quine, G. (eds), *Our Fragile Heritage. Documenting the Past for the Future,* The National Museum of Denmark, DKC, 1999, pp. 155–164.

3.   Hansen, H.J., 'Content, Use and Perspectives of DKC, the Danish National Record of Sites and Monuments', in Larsen, C.U. (ed), *Sites & Monuments. National Archaeological Records,* The National Museum of Denmark, DKC, 1992, pp. 23–42.

4.   Bruce-Mitford, R., *The Sutton Hoo Ship-Burial: a Handbook,* 1947 (third edition, 1979).

5.   Ólafsson, G., 'Recording standards for archaeological field surveys in Iceland', in Hansen, H.J. and Quine, G. (eds), *Our Fragile Heritage. Documenting the Past for the Future,* The National Museum of Denmark, DKC, 1999, pp. 75–82.

6.   See Changing Landscapes: www.ou.dk/Hum/ForandLand/Dansk/

7.   See Agrar2000: www.natmus.dk/Agrar2000/

8.   Palumbo, G., 'JADIS: a Sites and Monuments Record in Jordan', in Hansen, H.J. and Quine, G. (eds), *Our Fragile Heritage. Documenting the Past for the Future,* The National Museum of Denmark, DKC, 1999, pp. 55–64.

9.   See DKC online: www.dkconline.dk/

10. Müller, S. et al, *Affaldsdynger fra Stenalderen i Danmark,* C. A. Reitzel, 1900.

11. Andersen, S.H., 'Køkkenmøddingerne - Ældre stenalders kystbopladser', in Nørgård Jørgensen, A. and Pind, J. (ed), *Før landskabets erindring slukkes – Status og fremtid for dansk arkæologi,* Rigsantikvaren & Det Arkæologiske Nævn, 2001, pp. 25–40.

13

CULTURAL LANDSCAPE AND SPATIAL PLANNING
England's Historic Landscape Characterisation Programme

Graham Fairclough

The idea that is summed up by the words 'historic landscape' or 'cultural landscape' embraces all of the physical remains of past human activity that create the palimpsest of today's environment and reveals the long story of cultural change and human decisions across several millennia. It can also include all of the intangible associations which people invest in their landscape. Yet despite its inclusivity and centrality to everyday life, the landscape is one of the least well understood and least-protected aspects of the cultural heritage. This is partly of course simply because it is so all encompassing. It seems also, however, to be because conservation's traditional view concerning individual sites and monuments creates a tendency to see it merely as background, discouraging a view of it as separate, and significant in its own right.

But it is in its own right that landscape is perhaps the most fundamental, the most diverse, and the most readily accessible of any part of the cultural heritage. It is human habitat, partly inherited from nature but extensively adapted to human needs by centuries and millennia of modification and change.[1] It is essential to social and personal health and to economic well-being, as evidenced by the social, economic and emotional problems that frequently accompany attempts to wipe the slate clean and create entirely new environments for people to live in. Some connection with the past seems to be essential. Looking after the historic environment, so that it can be used to manage change, is therefore a necessary goal.

As in any branch of conservation and spatial planning, the first step to looking after the landscape is to have an understanding of what exists, how

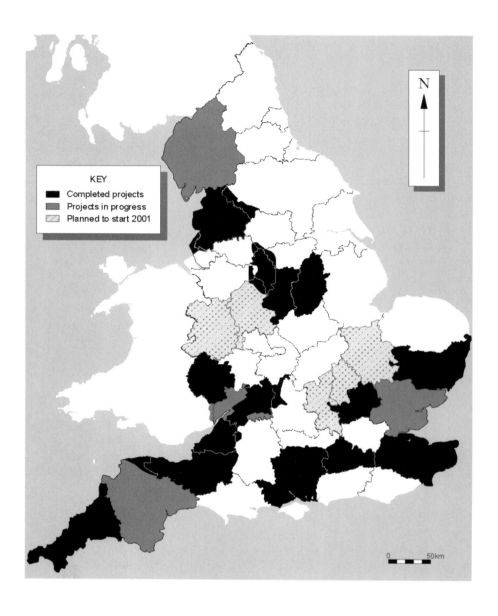

Figure 1 Progress with Historic Landscape Characterisation county projects at April 2001. *Drawn by Vince Griffin, English Heritage*

it works, and what its significance is. For the landscape as a whole this is precisely what is most lacking. The historic landscape has been taken for granted by conservation and planning. It has been overlooked because it is everywhere. Its size and complexity, compared to the more straightforward business of identifying and evaluating separate sites, monuments and buildings, is its greatest challenge.

During the past decade, English Heritage (EH) has been looking at ways to meet this challenge, and since 1993, in partnership with local government archaeologists, has been developing ways of bringing historic landscape to the forefront of conservation.[2,3,4] This has happened as part of a broader trend towards understanding better the whole of the historic landscape.[5,6,7,8,9,10] It has also happened as part of a move to look at the landscape from a wide range of other viewpoints.[11,12,13,14,15]

The present paper describes the national programme that has emerged over the past decade and is now approaching its halfway point of Historic Landscape Characterisation (HLC) (Figure 1). Its products are county-wide GIS databases, capable of producing a wide range of characterisation maps and analysis, as well as being used to answer both strategic and site-specific planning questions. They have many functions and aims, from providing a summary of the current state of understanding (explicitly provisional, a starting point) to creating a platform for future research. One of their principal aims, however, is to provide information for conservation-led decision-making and for managing change in the historic environment. Spatial planning (here taken to include landscape strategy and agri-environmental incentive strategies as well as development plans and development control) is therefore a key delivery mechanism, on which this paper focuses in particular because of its relevance to the InterReg IIC 'Kings of the North Sea' project. The paper is one of a trilogy presented to conferences in the spring of 2001;[16,17] together these describe the evolution and current shape of Historic Landscape Characterisation and its applications, following more theoretical discussion of the general concept in earlier papers.[18,19,20,21]

As well as looking specifically at cultural landscape and spatial planning, this paper also illustrates many other themes relevant to the 'Kings of the North Sea' project that are most easily exemplified at landscape scale, but which apply to all parts of the historic environment, such as:

- how to provide the sound, accessible, and updateable information that is needed for managing any part of the historic environment, whether at landscape or site level;
- the importance of attempting to manage change everywhere, rather than only protecting special places and monuments;
- the advantages (beyond the ability to manage the landscape itself) of a landscape-scale understanding because it provides the necessary

framework for looking after individual sites and monuments and their settings;

- the benefits of integration and partnership taking all environmental aspects into account together, rather than looking separately at individual components, for example, ecology or buildings; bringing social issues into the equation alongside the more obvious economic drivers; working with others concerned with environmental and conservation issues; bridging across sectors, notably natural or cultural, and between institutional layers, national or regional with local for instance.

FOR THE FUTURE NOT THE PAST

Historic Landscape Characterisation (HLC) is a way of looking at landscape from an archaeologist's perspective. This is of course only one among many possible perceptions, including aesthetic, ecological and associative, but it has particular advantages. Most other approaches have little or no regard either for time-depth or for the cultural layers within landscape. The archaeological perspective by contrast pays particular attention to culture: the depth of time that can be read in the landscape, the existence within the present shape of the landscape of the remains of previous landscapes, the evidence for change as well as continuity. Above all, it insists upon the central role of people shaping our inherited landscape over very long spans of time.

It is this human and cultural dimension of landscape that distinguishes 'landscape' from 'environment'. This is what Historic Landscape Characterisation seeks to find and give value to, in order to manage future change, and to enable us to add a further richness to the landscape by cultural action or social transformation, as our predecessors always did.

The landscape of a country such as England, or a continent such as Europe, did not appear purely through natural processes, nor did the bio-diversity that it supports. Both have reached us through layer upon layer of human modification, destruction or improvement. This is why we talk of 'cultural landscape'. Cultural landscape may be ugly as well as beautiful, disturbing as well as comforting, fragmented and broken as well as homogenous and harmonious. It is never 'timeless' and it is almost never (at least in England) wholly natural. What defines it is the extent to which it is created by human processes through history.

Historic Landscape Characterisation is thus concerned particularly to understand the effect on the present day landscape of peoples' actions, and all the social and cultural change brought about by the passage of time. There are of course geographical and environmental determinants too. But they are not as dominant as is often claimed, and in any case they have a reciprocal relationship to earlier human modifications. It is of relatively limited interest simply to list the contribution of geology, soil or terrain, rather than to explore the infinitely richer if more subtle changes that have been wrought by culture and society.

The results of peoples' decisions and actions across many centuries are still clearly visible everywhere in the landscape. All parts of the landscape thus have their own distinctive character that testifies to history, stands witness to previous human achievements or failures, and guides the future possible shape of the landscape. The challenge for conservation and spatial planning is not to decide which parts of the landscape are most 'important' (which is quite simple) and should remain unchanged if possible (a more difficult task). The true challenge is to influence all the decisions that are made daily – and more importantly that are being made everywhere – about how much of yesterday's world is retained, and in what form, within tomorrow's landscape.

To rise to this challenge requires understanding and appreciation of the historic dimension everywhere, not just in the best areas; it also requires recognition that the goal is normally the flexible management of change, rather than total preservation.[22] The primary lesson of sustainable development should be the need to be careful with the inheritance from the past, of whatever type it is, whether clean air, whales or our own historic habitat. Managing change to the historic environment is part of the core definition of spatial planning, even though it rarely rises very high up spatial planning agendas and strategies, whether at European or regional level.

The European Union (EU) framework for looking after cultural heritage, although improving, is not strong. The EU's *European Spatial Development Perspective* recognises the historic environment as part of the natural and cultural environment, and that it is a common cultural asset which when carefully protected and managed makes a massive contribution to European diversity, identity, quality of life, economy and culture.[23] So do its regional follow-ups such as *NorVision* and *A Spatial Vision for North-West Europe* produced by Interreg IIC projects for the North Sea Region and the North-West Metropolitan Area.[24,25] Beyond this, however, these documents scarcely go further than merely registering the need for protecting special heritage places. Furthermore, they do this in isolation, mainly as part of the third component of the sustainable development triad of social, economic and environmental factors. This fails to recognise that care of the historic environment, and its sustainable use as an unparalleled resource, needs to be woven through the whole of sustainable development, not just within an environmental agenda. A truly sustainable approach requires close integration between all three factors (the social, the economic and the environmental), to the extent that they cannot really be separated in practical terms.

Correcting these shortcomings, and placing the historic environment as an asset at the centre of all spatial planning, could be one of the main tasks for projects implementing *NorVision* and moving on to the next generation of thinking on ESDP and sustainable development. Fortunately, there is now a good framework for doing this, in the Council of Europe's European Landscape Convention, launched at Florence in September 2000, but not yet in force, even though rapidly signed within 6 months by over 20 countries.[26] The Convention builds on several of the Council of Europe's family of conventions, notably Granada and Valetta, and on an earlier recommendation on cultural landscape areas.[27] It also makes valuable connections to Conventions and Directives on the natural environment.

In the European Landscape Convention there is no question of landscape being only a matter of aesthetic interpretation (landscape as scenery), or only a place valued because it supports animals, or only special places of whatever sort. Landscape is comprehensively defined, in very simple terms, as: 'an area, as perceived by people, whose character is the result of the action and interaction of natural and/or human factors'.

In this short, flexible and multi-purpose definition, the key words that put cultural and historic landscape at its centre are *action* and *interaction* (change and modification, in other words, by people). The manner in which landscape is doubly cultural is also enshrined within the definition. It is captured by the words human factors (landscape is cultural because its material remains have been made by people) and perception (landscape is cultural because it has to be imagined and understood by people before it ceases to be merely 'environment' and becomes landscape). Finally, it is significant that the definition speaks of an area's 'character', not of the land itself or its components. 'Character' is the construct that is built up from the mixture of physical remains, associations and ideas by those observing, interpreting and perceiving landscape.

The Florence Convention also sees that landscape exists everywhere: urban as well as rural, maritime as well as terrestrial, 'degraded' as well as well-preserved, everyday as well as outstanding. It is everywhere because (unlike 'environment') it resides mainly inside peoples' perception, and because, above all, it is everyone's common and personal heritage. A strong theme of democratic involvement runs through the Convention, recognising that democratic participation is essential to managing, preserving and using it wisely so that all its potential benefits can be released.

The Convention lists many of these potential benefits:

• its quality and diversity is a common resource of wide public interest
• it is a basic component of European heritage but it also forms local and regional culture
• it can create greater unity across Europe
• it is favourable to economic activity and jobs.

Such a benefit-based approach underlies the idea of Environmental and Quality of Life Capital, the practice of evaluating places and assigning significance not merely on the basis of their intrinsic qualities ('values') but more widely and constructively on the basis of their attributes. Identifying attributes (or affordances, the services or pleasures that places afford to their users) is a way of measuring what a place offers to cultural, social and economic use.[28,29]

HISTORIC LANDSCAPE CHARACTERISATION

Context
All of that – the guidance of Florence and its precursors and siblings, the framework provided by ESDP and its regional action plans – is part of the broad context into which the Historic Landscape Characterisation programme fits. So too are the debates about the historic environment's relevance to sustainable development,[30] managing change rather than preservation,[31] and democratic and personal participation.[32]

   In national terms, the context of the programme is also a desire to move on from the tradition of single-monument protection. It builds on the success of this traditional approach, which though effective in its own terms has nonetheless taken sites out of their context and protected them as islands with limited attempts to influence or manage the way their surrounding have been changing. Even when concerns for setting and context began to be addressed in the 1980s, new approaches fell short of looking at the historic significance and archaeological meaning of the whole landscape. In the later 1990s, for example, a degree of protection was introduced in the United Kingdom for field boundaries, one of the distinguishing marks of the English landscape. But protection was principally focused on the ecological value of hedges (and not walls or fences), which is a secondary attribute, rather than on their primary historic, archaeological or landscape values. The historic landscape, just as much of an artefact of human action and creation as, say, a church, house, town or prehistoric settlement, was still not treated in unified terms, nor in its own right, and this is what Historic Landscape Characterisation is designed to redress.

Concepts
Some of the principal concepts that support the philosophy and methodology of Historic Landscape Characterisation can be explained as follows:

a)   The whole landscape is a human artefact, to be studied and understood in cultural terms. This involves primarily studying today's landscape, not past landscape because historic landscape character exists in the here-and-now, not in the past. The study of past landscapes is important too, but it is a separate activity, and the best way to conserve the remains of past landscape is to have an effective way of managing the historic character of the existing landscape within which they sit.

b)   Primary place in explaining and understanding landscape character should go to people not to nature; this is not to deny that the environment has determined human actions, but to claim that it is most interesting for us, as people, to know about human impact on landscape, and thus its cultural and social dimensions, than it is to re-visit self-evident notions of environmental determinism.

c)   Although the landscape is made up of physical objects – such as buildings, hedges, walls, farms, woodland, or sites – it is only when viewed through perception, memory, imagination and ideas that these things come together to be landscape. Landscape is first and foremost interpretation and perception, an idea rather than a thing. It therefore has multiple meanings and diverse values; decisions about its future therefore call for very wide democratic discussion.

d)   The most important single attribute of landscape is, and always has been, change. The historic landscape today remains essentially dynamic and transient; protecting it is therefore primarily a question of managing change from a position of understanding about the history of that change. Knowing about change, understanding its causes and being able to identify its trajectory and speed are the basis for good, informed decisions about the future shape of the landscape. This recognition of the role of change – sometimes referred to in terms of 'living landscape' – should be one of the foundations of sustainable conservation and sustainable development.

HLC is designed first and foremost to bring together in one place what we already know or can interpret about the historic landscape from an archaeologist's perspective, in order to make possible sustainable management of change and conservation. It uses modern GIS as a tool for sophisticated analysis and interrogation, but is not led by technology or data-collation: it rests firmly upon interpretation and perception, initially expert-led but hopefully to become more democratic. It is first of all a conservation-led technique, designed to ensure that the landscape itself is taken fully into account in decision-making. It takes the starting point that the historic landscape is important not merely as the setting for a building, not simply as the place where wildlife lives, but in its own right as a major – perhaps the most significant – aspect of the cultural heritage.[33]

Methods
The technique of HLC is basically very straightforward and simple, though it is capable of enormous sophistication and is extremely flexible (Figure 2).[34,35]

It works best on the sort of large scale where broad patterns above the detail of each place's unique differences can be identified. It is desk-based, or rather computer-based, with very little fieldwork beyond some early

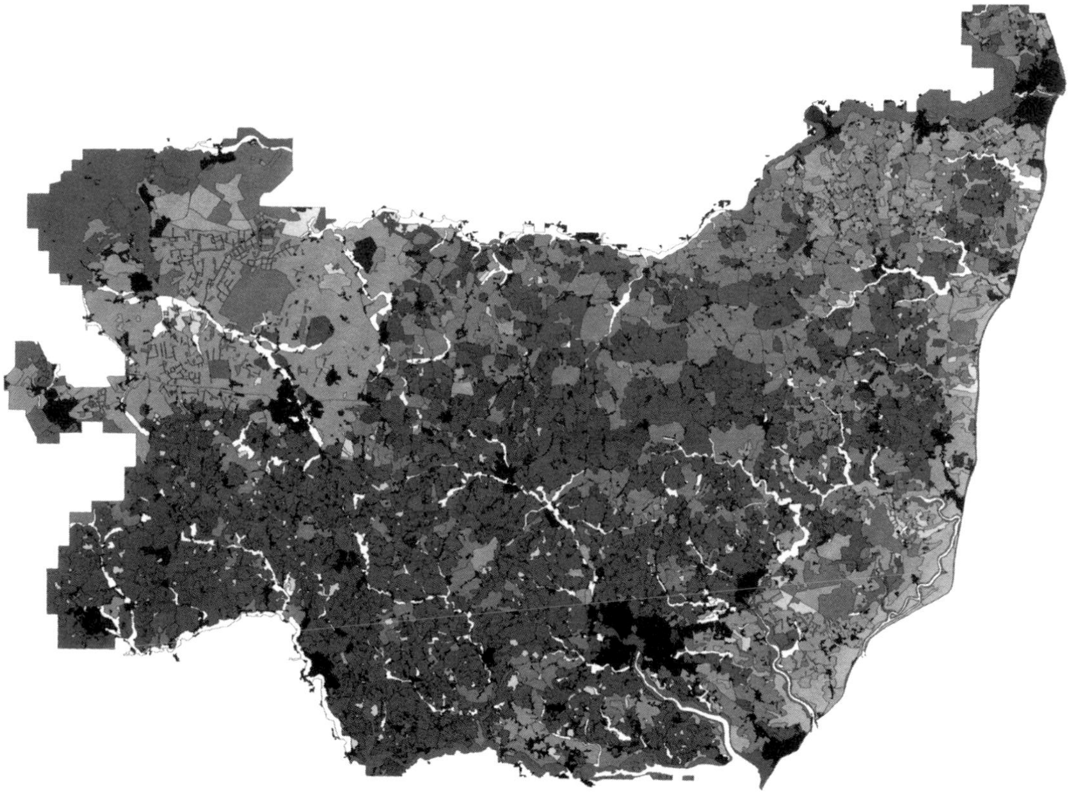

Figure 2 An example of a HLC map – Somerset (SW England). *Drawn by Oscar Aldred, Somerset County Council*

validation, because it synthesises known information as the starting point for later, more detailed, analysis or research. Having said that, it manages to produce new and sweeping interpretations of the historic dimension (whatever its date) of a whole county's landscape. One of the most important sources is the modern 1:10,000 or 1:25,000 map, showing field boundaries, buildings, and all land parcels. These maps are supported by up to date vertical air photos, other data-sets, preferably digital, on habitats or woodland, and to some extent historic maps, although they are rarely the first starting point because this is an archaeological not a historical approach.

To produce the characterisation, all areas of the modern landscape, through maps and air photos, are simply attributed to a range of 'historic landscape types', sometimes directly but more usually in more recent projects by recording the attributes (indicators or 'proxies') that allow high-level interpretation and analysis. Such attributes might include for instance enclosed land, the straightness or sinuosity of boundaries, the size of fields, the existence of dog-legs indicative of removed boundaries, the morphological signs of enclosed strip fields, or the pattern of cumulative assart from woodland. For industrial land, it might include whether it is extractive or manufacturing industry. Data is also recorded on the likely earlier form of landscape character, so that change through time can be studied. Information is also recorded on data sources, and on the strength of confidence of interpretation. There is a high degree of generalisation, so that the principal aspects of character for each area are defined rather than the detail of every distinct place. All these attributes are recorded against areas of land – GIS polygons – whose size and shape tends to follow the scale of the landscape.

Character is not usually defined for every land parcel or field, but for groups of land parcels, and thus the resolution of the map reflects and follows the landscape character. GIS polygons tend to be large in areas of great homogeneity (upland moorland for instance, unless sub-divided by, for example the presence/absence of visible medieval or prehistoric remains), but smaller in areas of greater diversity. Sites or areas of archaeology are not plotted as point data, or as realistic representations. Such information exists elsewhere in Sites and Monuments Records and can be used later against the base-map that HLC provides. It is this that distinguishes HLC from other approaches to studying archaeological landscape – it does not aim to plot the components of the landscape but to map a generalised depiction of its overall historic landscape character.

Defining Character
Historic landscape character is defined very broadly. Archaeological sites and buildings are not excluded from the process, but they are not mapped as such because they become a minor aspect when seeking to be an area-based generalised view of the landscape. Data about individual sites in the Sites and Monuments Record (SMR) can be superimposed later. This allows an

132

independent landscape characterisation to illuminate our understanding of site distribution, while also enabling new types of area data to be generated from site data, a process which seems to have been largely impossible until now. This process can enable the 'fingerprint' of an area's archaeological character to be drawn – the type of sites that can be expected here, and that might be expected to survive given later landscape change, or the combination of different types of sites (or predicted sites) that make up the area's identity.

More important than sites for HLC, therefore, are the broad pattern of the landscape, and the historic reasons for this pattern, the historic processes that created the landscape's character. Where is heathland, woodland, moorland, arable pasture located, for example? How does its distribution match earlier distributions (if they are known), or does it reflect at all what might be termed 'natural' distributions? In much of England, for example, old woodland now survives only in narrow, steep sided valleys unused for arable or pasture, or at the margin of parishes or townships. This is often demonstrably a manufactured not a natural pattern. Settlement pattern also falls into this category, as in the regionally specific mixture of nucleation and dispersion, for example, or of clustered and scattered farmsteads. Overall patterns of field boundaries form a major part of HLC, and it is the character of fields that forms the backbone of the work and the opportunity for most further research, trying to answer the many questions that every HLC project raises.

Behind these broad patterns HLC endeavours to keep historic processes to the forefront in other ways. Like the historic landscape character itself, these processes have changed through time, as has the balance between them. The processes that form the substructure of the HLC database include using the land to provide food, exploiting it for raw material, such as timber, stone or minerals, creating the habitat that produced bio-diversity, using the land to establish and symbolise ownership or social control or establishing settlements in it. Most polygons in the GIS database record previous land-uses as well as current, and therefore by implication or interpretation the transition between them. These are relatively intangible items, however, and being able to map them through the medium of characterisation has been a major step forward.

Even less tangible, but still just within the capacity of HLC as it has been practised so far in its still-evolving form, is the question of territoriality, of space across the landscape.[36] Most non-historic landscape assessment (driven by more aesthetic or ecological appreciation) has as its target the definition of 'character areas', areas that share common traits, such as valley bottoms, upland, coastal, or clay plateaux. These are nearly always topographically defined (as, too often, are even the subsidiary types that comprise them) and therefore these follow the geological and geographical 'grain' of the landscape. Land-use at all periods however has been far more complex than this. In particular, communities have always needed access to a mixture of resources, from cereal-growing land to pasture to woodland to fishing. These resources are found in different topographical units, and territories, therefore, crossed the grain of the landscape, whether at parish/township scale where parishes cover several land-use zones, or at sub-regional level. There were also temporal solutions (seasonal transhumance, for example) and solutions by trade and exchange, which equally affected the landscape's appearance. The EH Rural Settlement Atlas moves us in the direction of understanding some of these cross-county connections, defining macro-scale cultural territories to help offset the environmental determinism that is implicit in the definition of many character areas.[37] But HLC maps with their more local levels of detail allow these patterns to be identified more readily.

Finally, there is the largely unexplored area of the intangible associations of landscape and of public perception, and the views of 'real' people whether residents, visitors or both. Everyone has a particular landscape in their daily experience, on their doorstep or further afield, or in their heart and mind. What constitutes landscape in this sense varies from person to person, and from time to time, however, and encompasses stories, associations, memories or myths as well as history and archaeology. All of these can be personal as well as collective, emotional as well as intellectual. HLC has so far not been able to engage with these difficult issues, and no obviously effective methodology has yet been isolated. Some experimentation is underway, notably as part of the Bowland/Lune project, the English part of an EU-funded Culture 2000 project called European Pathways to the Cultural Landscape.

Applications
One of the main stimuli for developing the HLC method in the early–mid 1990s was that the effective operation of archaeological resource management on a site-by-site basis in the spatial planning system through PPG16 did not extend to the wider landscape. For all of these areas of spatial planning there was a worrying inability, largely through lack of the right sort of information presented in an appropriate way, to ensure that the overall character of the historic landscape (rather than the archaeology of a site) could be taken into account.

Existing archaeological approaches did not by and large treat the current landscape itself as material culture or as something to be studied in its own right, but rather merely as a backdrop, often considered as a negative or inappropriate one. The necessary information for historically-sensitive spatial planning policies and programmes rarely existed. What little was known about the landscape's historic aspect was not collated in accessible databases, and it was not expressed in language that was accessible to planners or landscape managers. It was too site-based to be incorporated into the broad-based assessments of scenic and visual character that were becoming commonplace in the early 1990s; it was too concerned with what might once have existed (rather than what does exist now) to engage people concerned with decisions about the present landscape. As a result, the past dimension of landscape was being overlooked in landscape strategies, and most spatial planning policies for the landscape were drafted by those who were disinterested in recognising the landscape's history and archaeology, its time depth or its human and cultural origins as opposed to natural attributes.

HLC was, therefore, specifically designed to start remedying this by using a language of landscape rather than of site.

The programme and its products also do much else to deliver information and perception for landscape management. Notably they explain and contextualise site information (Sites and Monuments Records). They also provide a benchmark for ensuring future change, by creating a snapshot of the landscape and of our perception of it: both will change and the benchmark becomes crucial in measuring the direction, pace and character of change. They also of course make contributions towards forming and defining local and regional identity, and they can offer a forum for bringing together specialist as well as populist or personal perspectives on landscape.

INFORMING SPATIAL PLANNERS

Spatial planning, and more generally the taking of decisions on the future of the historic environment as part of sustainable development, is the main focus of this paper because there are many ways in which HLC can inform planning.[38,39] For example, the value of characterisation for spatial planning is established in England within government planning guidance in PPG7 and PPG15.[40,41] The HLC GIS databases can provide information ('Supplementary Planning Guidance' in the English jargon) to support local and county development planning, thus providing a framework within which the impact and effect of individual development proposals can be judged. This might concern siting: for example, where new homes could be built, and in what manner, that most fits in with historic landscape character? New housing could be spread loosely across the landscape in areas of dispersed settlement where the whole landscape, from fields to roads, has for centuries been predicated on scattered settlements, or they could be added to existing nucleation of settlements where those exist. It might be that new towns represent a better way that fits in with landscape character, for example in dispersed areas where the characteristic focal market-towns faded away in the late Middle Ages, but still left the landscape infrastructure to support them. At least one planning inquiry in England has rejected proposals for small new settlements in inappropriate locations partly on the basis of arguments using historic landscape character.

The HLC databases can also be used to create views of the landscape that guide future change. They can tell us about recent landscape change that we might wish to reverse, or (more constructively) about current directions of change that we might wish to encourage or guide in some ways (eg reversion of pasture back to uplands at the hillside margin). Understanding historic landscape character for example might justify allowing change whilst leaving our successors with some visible trace of the past in their new landscape by ensuring for example that historic, but temporary, enclosures survive in some form (earthwork, ruined walls for example, not needing expensive maintenance like standing but non-functional walls).

HLC identifies attributes such as rarity, condition and completeness. Such information can guide us in deciding which areas to prioritise for investment in preservation and management, for instance through CAP-related agri-environmental incentives to farmers, as well as through development control. In Hertfordshire (part of an East Anglian HLC programme within the InterReg North Sea Region), the limited surviving extent and distribution of medieval or earlier field patterns and hedges can be defined, and its sub-regional significance appreciated.[42] There is, for example, a distinction between common-arable field types in the north of the county, and separate farms and earlier field patterns in the west and south. This exists at local level but also as part of the much broader landscape patterns revealed by the Rural Settlement Atlas.[43] To the east newer major patterns can be recognised in the new late twentieth-century 'prairie'-style landscapes that run eastwards into East Anglia.

Hedges and walls, and field patterns in general, are highly characteristic features of the English landscape and therefore a particularly important feature of HLC. Other European regions would need to use different indicators if they were to adopt HLC's basic approach and methods. But in England a focus on field boundaries has worked well, and means that HLC can now fill the gap that was evident when the first Hedgerow Protection Regulations were first introduced in 1997. The Regulations, and the operational criteria that informs them, tended to value hedges individually, for example by asking whether an individual hedge possessed a wide variety of tree species, or supported bird and animal populations, or was also a parish boundary. They were weak however on the landscape contribution of hedges, and on a hedge's value in relation to the whole system of which they were part. It is precisely this on which HLC focuses, because of its area rather than point basis. HLC allows an individual hedge to be given value because of its context, and in terms of its county-wide (and eventually regional and nation-wide) currency in terms of criteria such as rarity or relative condition. It also allows the likely date of a single hedge to be estimated on the basis of the morphology of the whole pattern. This escapes the reliance on documents and maps that has limited understanding both of the earlier phases of landscape, and of aspects of later landscape character that were only very partially documented.

More widely, HLC can easily be assimilated into holistic landscape management alongside other aspects of the landscape such as its ecological component, or the scenic and aesthetic attributes that are sometimes regarded as the whole landscape, rather than just one subset.[44,45] There are already a number of examples of this integration, and the number is growing.[46,47]

In operational and institutional terms, the reason why HLC is so rapidly beginning to influence spatial planning and landscape management is because they are deeply embedded into Sites and Monuments Records (SMRs). SMRs are the bedrock of English archaeology resource management. They are maintained by county councils or equivalent planning authorities and staffed by archaeologists. They are located within (or very close to) spatial planning departments, usually alongside countryside and biological sections. HLC projects therefore (although centrally initiated and mainly funded by English Heritage) are a local function maintained in SMRs alongside all the other records of aspects of the historic environment. They are consulted continuously by local and county planners, by farm advisers, landscape managers, the general public and researchers. SMRs hold much other data, such as information on archaeological sites or buildings, the results of urban archaeological assessments, the documentation of scheduled (legally-protected) monuments, historic maps (increasingly also GIS-based) or archaeological air photographs and the data plotted from them. All this can be combined with HLC maps to amplify its own essentially modern-day (or post-medieval) emphasis. More significantly, and at first surprising to some people, the HLC maps become a more useful and more meaningful base-map than the plain Ordnance Survey ('cadastral') land maps. They provide an intelligent matrix to contain SMR data, holding archaeological significance in relation to pattern of survival and condition.

For supplying information at a general level, two of the most interesting and useful ways of using HLC are to produce maps and analysis that

- first, allow the distribution and proportion of any type of historic landscape character to be considered, and
- second, demonstrate the character and rate of change to the landscape.

The first way is relatively simple (Figure 3). The HLC maps, for example, allow us to say in broad terms (that is, at landscape scale – different perceptions will usually prevail at site level) that n% of a county's land area has the character of eighteenth or nineteenth century field patterns, and that nn% is woodland. This allows comparison between areas, both between counties and more importantly within counties. The character of a district or parish in relation to its neighbours, can be described in the same way, by diagrams or maps showing the different types of historic landscape in each area, as well as being expressed in words and descriptions. All this provides a solid basis for starting to formulate forward-looking spatial plans and to exercise control over proposed development.

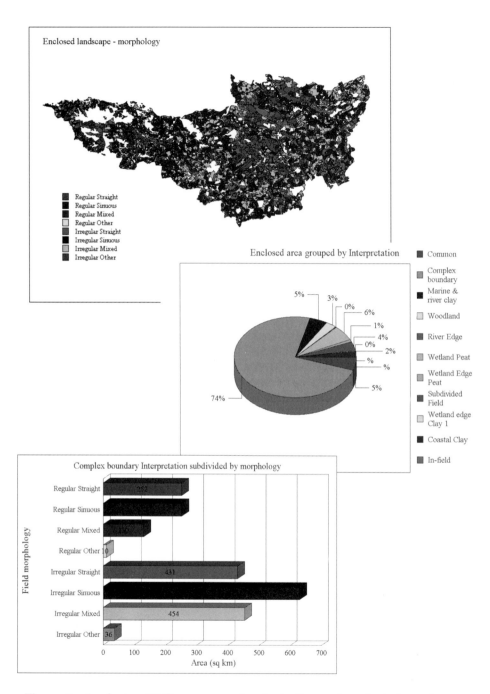

Figure 3 Analysing HLC – an example of selection and analysis from the GIS, Somerset. *Drawn by Oscar Aldred, Somerset County Council*

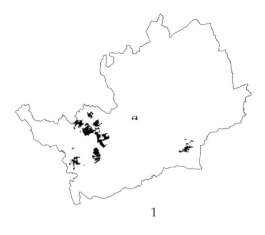

1

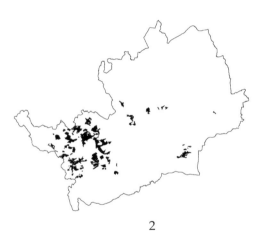

2

Figure 4   Defining chronology – Hertfordshire (E England, a series of maps showing (cumulatively) early (medieval or earlier) types of field systems.
Map 1: 'co-axial' fields only.
Map 2: 'co-axial' fields and fields with 'sinuous' boundaries. (from original analysis made by Lynn Dyson Bruce, Essex County Council; the maps represent work in progress, and in particular NE Hertfordshire is unfinished)

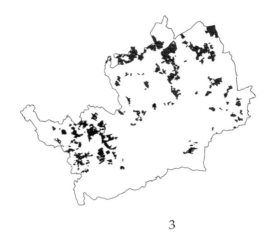

3

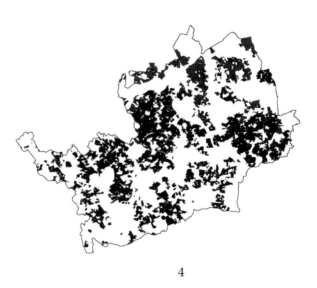

4

Figure 4 continued   Map 3: field types shown on Figures 1 and 2 plus
'common arable' fields.
Map 4 : field types shown on Figures 1, 2 and 3 plus all other undifferentiated
fields of 'irregular' shape. (from original analysis made by Lynn Dyson Bruce,
Essex County Council; the maps represent work in progress, and in particular
NE Hertfordshire is unfinished)

The second way is more complex, and there are many ways to achieve it. In one exercise, for example, the Hertfordshire map has been broken down into a series of cumulative layers that together build up to the map of the whole, present-day current landscape. The series starts with earlier medieval fields in a few areas (Figure 4), adds later, more common types, then designed parkland, urban expansion and so on. The same sort of modelling of how the landscape has grown can be done in reverse, or it can be 'time-sliced'. The Kent and Surrey HLCs in South-East England for example have been used to produce maps showing which areas at landscape scale have predominantly a twentieth or a nineteenth century overall character; or which at landscape scale show principally pre-1700 character (Figure 5). There is an important caveat here, however, since within these areas, an area of eighteenth century character can obviously at site scale also contain prehistoric or medieval remains. HLC must always therefore be used in conjunction with the other sources: it does not replace them, but complements them. It provides landscape scale perceptions for the first time ever, but they are perceptions that need to be added to other viewpoints. HLC was designed to fill the landscape gap in existing largely site-based records, and those records must still be used as well.

Another area in which HLC databases can be used is to measure rates of change. The most common method has been to produce comparisons between HLC and modern maps on the one hand and early or mid twentieth century maps on the other to measure boundary loss (mostly hedges) in enclosed land (Figure 6). The rate of loss and change are seen to be different in different areas, for a wide variety of reasons. Areas of highest loss correspond generally to the creation of new landscape types ('prairie' fields; new settlements; horticultural). The 'here-and-now' philosophy of HLC, however, allows us to treat this as the upper layer of the historic landscape, an addition to the landscape's character rather than only as the loss of something earlier. Some of these landscapes are now being valued on their own terms.

More refined analysis can reveal the direction and pace of change as well, whether in relation to the suburban sprawl of cites into their hinterland, the twentieth century retreat from cultivation at the upland edges, or the intensification and restructuring of lowland agriculture. Much of this work will require additional research, notably with earlier twentieth-century maps and air photos, but it is the HLC base-map that makes such work possible, provides a measuring point, and through HLC's links with spatial planning carry it into the decision-making realm.

None of this, of course, automatically tells planners or other decision-makers whether one area is more valuable or important than another. HLC is neutral in that sense, but it tells us what is there and why. Deciding what matters most, and for what reasons and to whom, and deciding what should happen to it, are a more complex series of decisions that need to draw in many more interests than just the archaeological if it is to be sustainable. It is also most

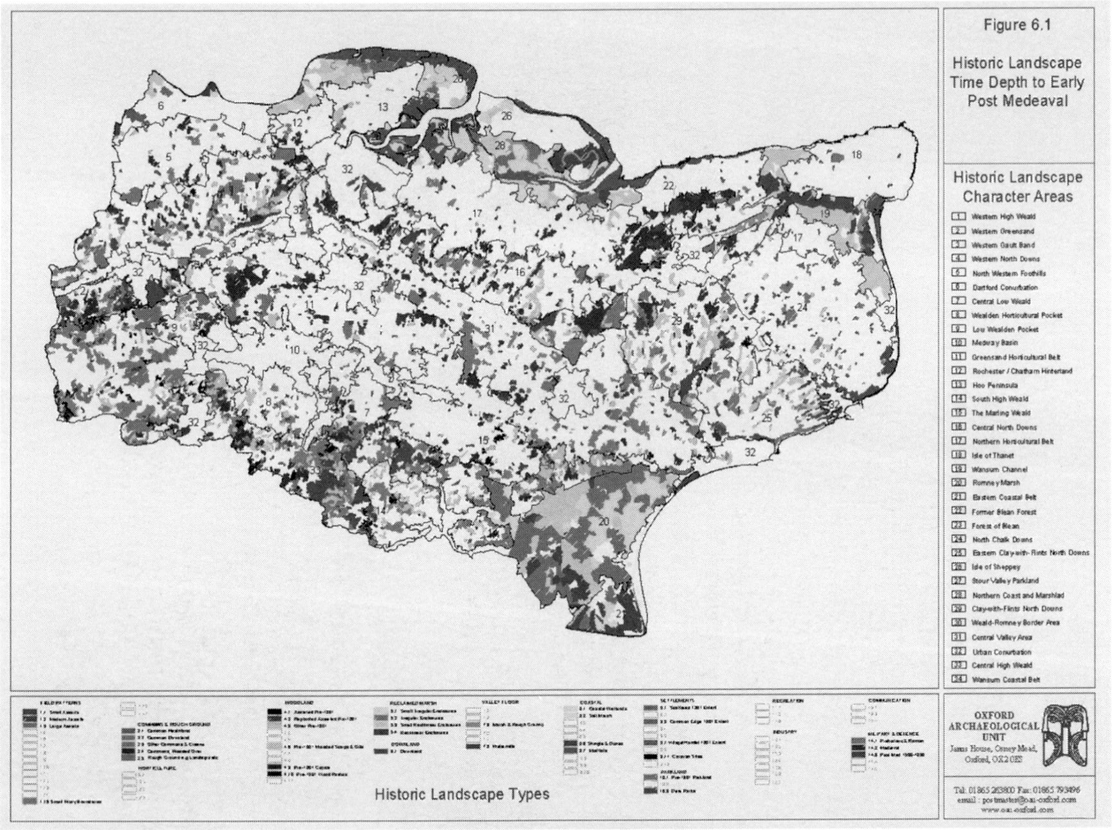

Figure 5 Time-depth – Kent (SE England), map from GIS showing areas whose historic landscape character probably predates c.1700. *Drawn by Oxford Archaeological Unit, Kent County Council*

142

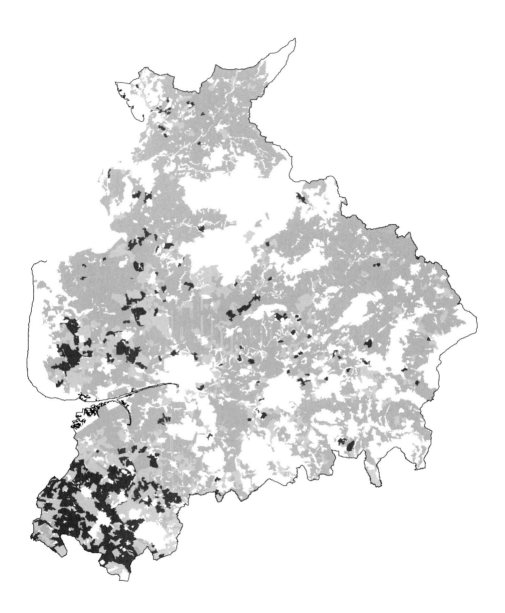

Figure 6 Measuring rates of change – Lancashire (NW England), degrees of field boundary (hedges) removal during the twentieth century. *Drawn by Joy Ede, Lancashire County Council*

effective when done in the context of specific proposals, so that evaluation becomes impact-led, opportunity-based and realistic, rather than quality-led and abstract. In some areas, and in the face of certain types of proposed change, late twentieth century landscapes might be judged more valuable than eighteenth century ones: the oldest landscape is not necessarily always the most important. But the all-important first stage – knowing what is there, being able to start to explain it, providing the basis for decisions – is carried out by HLC, and by the related techniques used by others' disciplines and sectors to assess the ecological, scenic or other facets of landscape character.

HLC also facilitates further research into the archaeological resource itself. The Bowland/Lune Valley project (the Culture 2000 European Pathways to the Cultural Landscape programme) will experiment with ways of using HLC to interrogate and better understand the SMR and other site-based data. Comparing HLC to SMR data in various parts of the country is already illustrating important new patterns and their meaning. It also helps to distinguish between patterns caused on the one hand merely by the distribution of fieldwork and its techniques, and on the other by the 'real' patterns of existence or survival.[48] Survival and 'visibility' are not absolutes. The right techniques can make visible the invisible, if we first know there is something to find and what sort of overlying layers of landscape we need to look through. Using HLC can therefore help to develop better predictive modelling tools for finding new sites, and thus facilitating spatial planning and development control.

HLC also provides a starting point for new, more data-led work. The Suffolk (and neighbouring) HLC has provided a broad picture of the diversity of historic field patterns and enclosure. The Settlement Atlas complements this, and on the basis of both, a two year research project was inaugurated by EH's Monuments Protection Programme with the SMRs in the area. This hopes to use historic documentation in a sample of 12 parishes or townships to generate a series of 'fingerprints' for different types of enclosure history that might be used with HLC to deepen understanding of the historic landscape. The project (still in progress) is likely to provide valuable new information for landscape management and spatial planning.

One final dimension of measuring change is simply to demonstrate how far the 'time-less' aspect of the landscape is a myth. Much cherished landscape – England's National Parks for example, such as the Lakes (North-West England) with its picturesque views and patterns of enclosed walls between, or the Derbyshire Peak District (south Pennines, within Interreg North Sea Region), with its white-walled pasture landscape, belie their long history of change. Both the Lakes and the Peak District are merely a few centuries old in their essential present landscape character, yet great amounts of earlier archaeology, and landscape features still survive if sought out. The customary tourist-centred view of these places, for example, overlooks many highly visible remains of the past. These include once-extensive high-altitude prehistoric and medieval farming, or the noisy, environmental destruction of stone, copper and lead mining, still easily observed as archaeological sites, or the quite different but still legible medieval patterns that lie beneath the current field walls. In many places all these are sufficiently visible once they have been highlighted to be a major part of landscape character. HLC offers to deepen the interest of these places, to reveal a much longer story, to make the past relevant by underlining the fact that, like the present, the past was only transient, changing and never-fixed. We are not the first generation to have to grapple with massive and unsettling environmental and landscape change. It can be a healthy perspective to learn that the landscape change we are living through is not necessarily greater or more rapid than that our predecessors experienced. Trying to manage as well as prevent change to the cultural landscape provides an opportunity to continue the landscape's cultural evolution, and to shape its future while passing on part of the legacy we inherited: this, surely, is the essence of spatial planning.

ACKNOWLEDGEMENTS

First, most thanks as always to Liz Page, whose patience, forbearing and above all organisational skills made possible this paper, and much of the work it describes. Second, I must acknowledge all the people who worked on the county HLC projects (many but not all are mentioned in the Bibliography), who have contributed most to the development of HLC as a practical method; often I have felt merely an observer.

References

1. Fairclough, G.J., 'Landscapes From the Past – Only Human Nature', in Selman, P. (ed), *The Ecology and Management of Cultural Landscapes* (Proceedings of an IALE UK conference at Cheltenham 1993 published in *Landscape Issues, Journal of the Dept of Countryside and Landscape, Cheltenham College Vol 11 No 1*), 1994, pp. 64–72.
2. Fairclough, G.J., et al, *Yesterday's World, Tomorrow's Landscape: The English Heritage Historic Landscape Project 1993–94*, English Heritage, 1999.
3. Fairclough, G.J. (ed), *Historic Landscape Characterisation (Papers presented at an English Heritage seminar held at the Society of Antiquaries, 11 December 1998)*, English Heritage, 1999.
4. Fairclough, G.J., 'Boundless Horizons: Historic Landscape Characterisation', in *Conservation Bulletin, English Heritage*, Issue 40, March 2001, pp. 23–26.
5. Council of Europe, *Recommendation R(95)9 of the Committee of Ministers to Member States on the integrated conservation of cultural landscape areas as part of landscape policies*, 1995.

6.   Countryside Commission, *Views From the Past – Historic Landscape Character in the English Countryside*, consultation report, 1994.

7.   Countryside Commission, *Views From the Past – Historic Landscape Character in the English Countryside*, CCW4 (final version), 1996.

8.   Droste, B., et al (eds), *Cultural landscapes of universal value. Components of a Global Strategy*, 1995.

9.   Brown, I.W. and Berry, A.R. (eds), *Managing Ancient Monuments: An Integrated Approach*, Association of County Archaeology Officers/Clwyd County Council, 1995.

10.   Macinnes, L. and Wickham-Jones, C.R., *All Natural Things: Archaeology and the Green Debate*, Oxbow Monograph No 21, 1992.

11.   Countryside Commission, *Landscape Assessment Guidance*, CCP423, 1993.

12.   Countryside Commission, *Countryside Character*: vol 1 *North East* (CCP535), vol 2 *North West* (CCP536), vol 3 *Yorkshire and the Humber* (CCP536), 1998.

13.   Countryside Agency, *Countryside Character*: vol 4 *East Midlands* (CA10), vol 5 *West Midlands* (CA11), vol 6 *The East* (CA12), vol 7 *South-East* (CA13), vol 8 *South*-West (CA14), 1999.

14.   English Nature, *Natural Areas Profiles* (many volumes, and eight regional overviews available from English Nature local offices), 1997–8.

15.   English Heritage, Countryside Commission and English Nature, *Conservation Issues in Local Plans*, English Heritage, 1996.

16.   Fairclough, G.J., 'Cultural landscape, sustainability and living with change?', in *Proceedings of the US/ICOMOS 4th International Symposium, Philadelphia, April 5–8 2001*, forthcoming.

17.   Fairclough, G.J., 'Cultural landscape, computers and characterisation', in *Proceedings of the 2001 Computer Applications in Archaeology conference, Visby April 2001*, forthcoming.

18.   Fairclough, G.J., 'The Sum of All Its Parts : An Overview of the Politics of Integrated Management in England', in Brown, I.W. and Berry, A.R. (eds), *Managing Ancient Monuments: An Integrated Approach*, Association of County Archaeology Officers/Clwyd County Council, 1995, pp. 17–28.

19.   Fairclough, G.J. (ed), *Historic Landscape Characterisation (Papers presented at an English Heritage seminar held at the Society of Antiquaries, 11 December 1998)*, English Heritage, 1999.

20.   Fairclough, G.J., 'Protecting Time and Space: understanding historic landscape for conservation in England', in Ucko, P.J. and Layton, R. (eds), *The Archaeology and Anthropology of Landscape: Shaping your landscape*, One World Archaeology 30, Routledge, 1999, pp. 119–34.

21.   Fairclough, G.J., 'Protecting the Cultural Landscape – national designations and local character', in Grenville, J. (ed), *Managing the Historic Rural Environment*, Routledge/English Heritage, 1999, pp. 27–39.

22.   Fairclough, G.J., 'Cultural landscape, sustainability and living with change?', in *Proceedings of the US/ICOMOS 4th International Symposium, Philadelphia, April 5–8, 2001, forthcoming*.

23.   European Union, *European Statial Development Perspective*, 1999.

24.   NorVision Working Group, *NorVision, A Spatial Perspective for the North Sea Region*, 2000.

25. NWMA Spatial Planning Group, *A Spatial Vision for North-West Europe*, North-West Metropolitan Area, Interreg IIC Secretariat, 2001.
26. Council of Europe, *European Landscape Convention*, European Treaty Series – No 176, Florence, 2000.
27. Council of Europe, *Recommendation R(95)9 of the Committee of Ministers to Member States on the integrated conservation of cultural landscape areas as part of landscape policies*, Strasbourg, 1995.
28. Countryside Commission, English Nature and English Heritage, *What Matters and Why: environmental capital – a new approach*, Cheltenham, 1997.
29. Countryside Agency, English Heritage, English Nature and the Environment Agency, *Quality of Life Capital: Managing environmental, social and economic benefits, 2001.*
30. English Heritage, *Sustaining the historic environment, 1997.*
31. Fairclough, G.J., 'Place and locality a non-monumental heritage?', in *Proceedings of the Interpreting Historic Places Conference, York, 3–7 September, 1997*, Routledge, forthcoming.
32. English Heritage and the Historic Environment Review Steering Group, *Power of Place, 2000.*
33. Fairclough, G.J. et al, *Yesterday's World, Tomorrow's Landscape: The English Heritage Historic Landscape Project 1993–94*, English Heritage, 1999.
34. Fairclough, G.J. (ed), *Historic Landscape Characterisation (Papers presented at an English Heritage seminar held at the Society of Antiquaries, 11 December 1998)*, English Heritage, 1999.
35. Fairclough, G.J., 'Cultural landscape, computers and characterisation', in *Proceedings of the 2001 Computer Applications in Archaeology conference, Visby, April 2001*, forthcoming.
36. Fairclough, G.J., 'Protecting Time and Space: understanding historic landscape for conservation in England', in Ucko, P.J. and Layton, R. (eds), *The Archaeology and Anthropology of Landscape: Shaping your landscape*, One World Archaeology 30, Routledge, 1999, pp. 119–34.
37. Roberts, B.K. and Wrathmell, S., *An Atlas of Rural Settlement in England*, English Heritage, 2000.
38. Lambrick, G. and Bramhill, P., *Hampshire historic landscape assessment*, final report, vols 1 & 2, Oxford Archaeology Unit and Scott Wilson Resource Consultants for Hampshire County Council, 1999.
39. Fairclough, G.J. (ed), *Historic Landscape Characterisation (Papers presented at an English Heritage seminar held at the Society of Antiquaries, 11 December 1998)*, English Heritage, 1999, part 2.
40. Department of the Environment, *The Countryside – Environmental Quality and Economic and Social Development, Planning Policy Guidance (PPG) 7*, HMSO, 1997.
41. Department of the Environment and Department of National Heritage, *Planning and the Historic Environment, Planning Policy Guidance (PPG) 15*, HMSO, 1994, paragraphs 2.26 and 6.40.
42. Lynn Dyson Bruce, pers comm.
43. Roberts, B.K. and Wrathmell, S., *An Atlas of Rural Settlement in England*, English Heritage, 2000.

44.   Countryside Commission, *Landscape Assessment Guidance, CCP423*, 1993.
45.   Countryside Agency, *Landscape Character Guidance,* forthcoming.
46.   Lancashire County Council, *A Landscape Strategy for Lancashire,* 2000.
47.   New Forest District Council, *New Forest District Landscape Character Assessment: Main Report and Supplementary Annexes,* New Forest District Council, Hampshire County Council, the Countryside Agency and English Heritage, 2000.
48.   Herring, P., *Cornwall's Historic Landscape. Presenting a method of historic landscape character assessment,* Cornwall Archaeology Unit and English Heritage, CCC, 1998.

Further Reading

Aldred, O., *Somerset and Exmoor Historic Landscape Characterisation Project 1999–2000,* Somerset County Council and English Heritage, 2001.

Bannister, N., *Surrey Historic Landscape Characterisation,* Surrey County Council, English Heritage and the Countryside Agency, 2001.

Barnatt, J., *Landscape Through Time: Historic Landscape Characterisation in the Peak Park, draft report,* Peak District National Park Authority and English Heritage, 1999.

Barnatt, J., Johnson, M. and May, R., *The Derbyshire Historic Landscape Survey Character Assessment – Aims, Method and Definition of Character Types,* Peak District National Park Authority for English Heritage and Derbyshire County Council, 2000.

Bramhill, P. and Munby, J., *Kent Historic Landscape Characterisation Report,* Oxford Archaeology Unit/Kent County Council/English Heritage, 2001.

Bruce, L.D. et al, *Historic Landuse Assessment (HLA): Development and Potential of a Technique for Assessing Historic Landuse Patterns. Report of the pilot project 1996–1998,* Historic Scotland and the Royal Commission on the Ancient and Historical Monuments of Scotland, 1999.

Department of the Environment, *Archaeology and Planning, Planning Policy Guidance (PPG) 16,* HMSO, 1990.

Donachie, J. and Hutcheson, A., *The South-West Wiltshire Historic Landscape Character Assessment,* Wessex Archaeology, 2000.

Ede, J. with Darlington, J., *The Lancashire Historic Landscape Characterisation Project Report,* Lancashire County Council/English Heritage, 2001.

European Union, *European Spatial Development Perspective,* Potsdam, 2000.

Fairclough, G.J., 'Assessment and characterisation: English Heritage's historic landscape policy', in *Landscapes perception, recognition and management: reconciling the impossible?, Proceedings of a conference at Sheffield, 1996,* (Landscape archaeology and ecology, Vol 3, 1998), The Landscape Conservation Forum and Sheffield Hallam University, 1998.

Fairclough, G.J., 'Place and locality a non-monumental heritage?', in *Proceedings of the Interpreting Historic Places Conference, York, 3–7 September 1997,* Routledge, forthcoming.

148

Ford, M., *Historic Landscape Characterisation in East Anglia: Part 1 – Suffolk*, Suffolk County Council and English Heritage, 1999.

Grenville, J. (ed), *Managing the Historic Rural Environment*, Routledge/English Heritage, 1999.

Hoyle, J., *Historic Landscape Characterisation: Cotswolds AONB*, draft report by Gloucestershire County Council, 1999.

Miller, K.R., T*he Isle of Axholme Historic Landscape Characterisation Project*, Countryside Commission, 1997.

Roberts, B., and Wrathmell, S., *Region and Place: a study of English rural settlement*, English Heritage, forthcoming.

Selman, P. (ed), *The Ecology and Management of Cultural Landscapes* (Proceedings of an IALE UK conference at Cheltenham 1993 published – *Landscape Issues, Journal of the Dept of Countryside and Landscape*, Cheltenham College Vol 11 No 1), 1994.

Ucko, P.J. and Layton, R. (eds), *The Archaeology and Anthropology of Landscape: Shaping your landscape*, One World Archaeology 30, Routledge, 1999.

White, P., *The Herefordshire Historic Landscape Characterisation Report*, Herefordshire County Council and English Heritage, forthcoming.

14

PLANNING FOR EARLY MEDIEVAL SCULPTURE
The Recovery and Recognition of Sense, Place and Setting

Sally M Foster

Early medieval sculpture is by no means unique to Scotland, or indeed to the North Sea Region, but it is one of Scotland's principal cultural assets. This material is critical to our being able to understand the formative period of the Scottish nation from AD 450 to 1050. Through it we can gain a unique insight into the early medieval peoples of Scotland – the Britons, Gaels, Angles, Norse and, in particular, the Picts. It is all the more important in a period about which we otherwise know so little. How we choose to conserve, present and interpret it raises issues that are often peculiar to this type of cultural material. The starting point is the often contentious, and certainly problematic, question of where sculpture should be preserved and the issues that stem from the practice of retaining it *in situ,* or at least locally, wherever possible. The aim of this paper is to describe present policy and practice on the location of sculpture and to review the issues associated with putting such policy into practice. The history of the ideas underpinning present practice is described in detail elsewhere.[1]

   Historic Scotland is the government body responsible for the protection of the built heritage on behalf of the Scottish Ministers. Of the estimated 2000 plus early medieval sculptural fragments that survive, about 560 are afforded statutory protection (through our ancient monument rather than listed building legislation). Of these, we directly care for about 350, including most of the finest examples (Figure 1). No other body is responsible for as many or as important a collection of early medieval carvings in Scotland, if not the United Kingdom. In nearly all cases, the cultural significance of the sculpture in Historic Scotland's care is markedly enhanced by its continued association with its findspot.[2]

Figure 1 The eighth-century free-standing cross at Kildalton, Islay, a particularly fine sculpture in the care of Historic Scotland. *Crown copyright Historic Scotland*

In recognition of the responsibilities and opportunities we have in caring for such material, Historic Scotland is in the process of preparing an Interpretation Plan for early medieval sculptures in its care. At the same time we are revising, for public consultation in due course, an operational policy for carved stones of all types and periods, whether in state or private care and whether legally protected or not. I say revising, since we have been operating to widely discussed principles since our first ancient monument legislation in 1882, principles that have underpinned, for example, our public information leaflets on carved stones.[3,4,5]

My premise is that in providing interpretative provision for sculpture we have to treat it not simply as artistic treasure, albeit a highly significant part of the art of Christendom, but as a component in the broader historical landscape. Visitors can only begin to appreciate the meaning of the sculpture if they can fully understand its context as part of the fabric of the site and landscape, both past and present. It is therefore important that we see the sculpture, as far as possible, in or near to its findspot and that its modern environment is conducive to appreciation of this relationship.

Historic Scotland and its predecessor departments have always sought to ensure that the highest standard of conservation strategies and practices are adopted, and that these are in the best interests of the carved stone. The aim of the conservation of carved stones has been to retain their cultural significance whilst making provisions for their future needs, including security and maintenance. There is therefore a presumption in favour of retaining the physical association of sculpture with its original site. Where an upstanding sculpture is believed to be in its original location, the presumption is that it shall not be removed unless demonstrable conservation needs outweigh the significance of retaining the monument in its original archaeological, architectural or landscape setting.

This principle has not changed since the early days of the Ancient Monument Protection Act (AMPA) of 1882. In spite of that, Scotland has had over a century's history of contested and high-profile claims relating to the location of early medieval sculpture. But why? There is of course no single answer, each case is different and has to be set against its broader historical context, but common threads emerge. In the next part of this paper I will sketch some of the historical background. What emerges as the most common cause of tension is the schizophrenic identity of sculpture – whether it is treated as a monument or artefact – and the closely related question of its ownership.

MONUMENT OR ARTEFACT?

Prior to the late nineteenth century, involvement in monuments was largely the concern of interested private owners and private societies. This was to change in 1882 when the first State legislation was introduced to protect ancient monuments. This led to a collision of respective interests between the predecessor bodies of the National Museums of Scotland and Historic Scotland. The thorny issue in the late 1880s/early 1890s was that of the fate of early medieval carved stones.

In 1882 moveable sculptures, such as had previously been presented to, or acquired by, the National Museum of Antiquities, came within the scope of the AMPA 1882. This led to a public debate about where sculpture should be curated, a dialogue that is documented in the writings of Joseph Anderson, the museum curator, and General Pitt Rivers, the first Inspector of Ancient Monuments for the British Isles.[6,7,8,9,10] Both parties shared a concern to preserve the sculpture but had completely different views on whether it was preferable to do so in a centralised museum or to retain an association with the findspot, *in situ* if possible.[11] Pitt Rivers' views can be summarised as follows:[12]

- A reluctance to deprive country places of their old associations and of things that draw people to visit them. This was also expressed in terms of robbing or sacrificing country places in the interests of towns and foreigners.
- Minor monuments could be overlooked if collected together with others in an over-crowded museum.
- The pattern of local diversity would be less obvious if the stones were not retained locally.
- Owners could not be obliged under the legislation to give their monuments to a museum so the danger was that a centralised collection would never be representative.
- It would be impossible to fund the building of a museum large enough to contain all of Scotland's early medieval sculpture.
- If public interest was not generated in such monuments then there would be no pressure on government to fund necessary works to protect them.

Pitt Rivers had developed these ideas in the context of local proposals to move the Pictish stones at Dyce (City of Aberdeen) 6 km away to Aberdeen. He considered that they should not lose their association with the church site on which they were found, and that a part of the church should be maintained for their preservation. To cut a long story short, the stones were retained on site, but because of problems about who was going to be responsible for the building and the difficulty of finding funds to repair it, the church was de-roofed by the local community and only a small shelter was built to protect the sculpture.

Dyce throws up issues that are in many senses still typical of casework associated with this material:

- How and where to preserve material on site.

- The implications of preserving sculpture in a historic building. Is the space suitable for the optimum display of the sculpture? Is the historic building structurally sound and who will have responsibility for maintaining this?
- Different perceptions of how local 'local' is or need be.
- The difficulties of getting an appropriate local party to take responsibility for a site.
- The difficulty of reconciling the various interests and priorities of different parties.

FRAGMENTED IDENTITY, FRAGMENTED ADMINISTRATION

If there continues to be a tension between museum curators, cultural resource managers and the wider public about the fate of early medieval sculpture, the reason can commonly be found in identity of this material and how this is reflected in the legislation. Arguably all early medieval sculpture was conceived of by its patron and maker as a monument in its own right – a gravemarker, prayer cross, etc – or as part of a monumental structure, such as an architectural feature within a church. But on the basis of its present form and context, sculpture is variously treated as either monument or artefact (a formal distinction that would not have been recognised in this way in the late nineteenth century).

New discoveries from excavations, etc are automatically treated as artefacts and subject to Treasure Trove to determine ownership. In the case of above-ground site-based material that is already known, the interpretation of the current legislation, the Ancient Monuments and Archaeological Areas Act 1979,[13] and indeed its predecessors, has always been problematic with regard to sculpture. Solicitors advising Historic Scotland have tended to take the view that at least part of an assemblage of sculpture should be earthfast to be eligible for either scheduling or to be taken into state care, not least since this has clarified the question of who might own it. The legislation *is* explicit that it is the 'situation of that object or its remains in that particular site' that has to be a 'matter of public interest' for scheduling to apply. In practice Historic Scotland has tended only to apply the legislation to sculpture that is fixed in some way to the ground or a structure, and therefore immoveable (meaning it can be appropriately recorded at Sasines). This is because the relationship to the place formally scheduled could otherwise be easily lost. Although not legally tested, there tends to be the presumption that if material which was fixed is moved it loses its formal protection under the ancient monuments legislation.

The danger is that in distinguishing between the management of elements of the same *corpus* of material on the grounds of whether it is legally a monument or artefact could obscure the fact that the *corpus* of sculpture needs to be considered as a whole. Different people in the same organisation, or more usually different organisations, will end up dealing with it. In practice this already happens, although the National Committee on the Carved Stones of Scotland, a body formed in 1993 with membership drawn from all national organisations, is a very useful additional means of communicating and counteracting some of this polarity.

The second obvious cause of difficulty is ownership, a subject closely related to legal status. All portable material recovered from the ground has to be declared Treasure Trove, in other words declared to the Crown so that it may have the opportunity to claim it. Any new finds of sculpture, whether from archaeological excavations or a chance discovery are therefore treated as artefacts and disposed of to an appropriate museum, invariably a local one, although tensions can arise if the most appropriate museum is distant from the site. This tends only to happen for one of three reasons. Firstly, if the museum in question was the legitimate recipient of a historic donation. This is because the presumption is that where an institution already holds the main collection of material from a site, it will be allocated new discoveries from it.[14] Newly discovered material from excavations at Tarbat, Portmahomack (Highland) has therefore been disposed to the National Museums of Scotland. However, the Museum's loan of both old and new finds to the newly-opened Tarbat Discovery Centre is an excellent model of how material can be displayed locally when the circumstances are appropriate. On the same basis the National Museums of Scotland can reasonably anticipate allocation of the newly discovered fragments of the Hilton of Cadboll cross-slab (Highland), for it was given the rest of the same sculpture in 1921. This impressive eighth century sculpture is now a prominent and key exhibit in the Museum of Scotland's *Early Peoples* gallery (Figure 2). We can therefore also reasonably anticipate that, if it is technically feasible, the National Museum will wish to physically reunite the fragments, and certainly to display them together. Arguments for splitting a single monument cannot be sustained on curatorial grounds – this is hardly in the best interest of the sculpture itself – but local provision of replica material is perhaps a reasonable expectation. As we are already beginning to see, this exciting new discovery cannot fail to provoke present-day sensitivities about the fact that the cross-slab is in Edinburgh at all. This contrasts with 1921 when the concern was not so much where it was displayed in Scotland, but the fact that it had been donated to the British Museum and had therefore left the country (it was returned to Edinburgh after high level protests).

The second reason today why material may not be disposed of close to home is that it can only be disposed of to museums that have met the minimum standards of registration set by the Scottish Museums Council and the most immediate museum may not yet be registered.

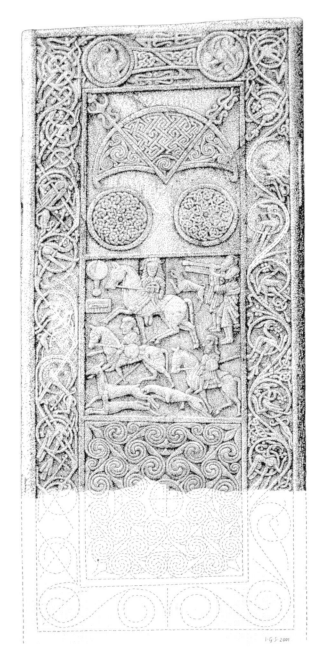

Figure 2 Ian G. Scott's drawing of the Hilton of Cadboll cross-slab, now in the Museum of Scotland. *Crown copyright Historic Scotland*

157

Thirdly, museums may seek to acquire new material that fills a significant gap in their collection, an action that will have first been determined in terms of an existing collection policy, approved in advance by the Scottish Museums Council.

The ownership of earthfast material visible above ground is unfortunately not always straightforward either. On non-church land it has never been legally questioned, to the best of my knowledge, that an earthfast sculpture belongs to the modern owner of the land. For example, Lord Forteviot received Inheritance Tax Exemption for transfer of the Dupplin Cross to state ownership despite the fact there was no reason to think that he was a relation of the Pictish king who had caused the monument to be erected. (It would, in any case, not be possible to identify with certainty modern heirs of the families who caused any early medieval sculpture to be made.) The Dupplin Cross is the rare example of a well-preserved, early ninth century, Pictish, free-standing cross. With its imagery explicitly relating to kingship at a pivotal time in the development of the Scottish nation, it is amongst the most important ninth-century monuments in Scotland. Since at least the late seventeenth century it is known to have stood on a hill overlooking the valley of the Earn, the site of the ninth century and later royal palace of Forteviot. When in 1994 the owner and the National Museum of Scotland submitted a joint proposal for the removal of the Cross, a scheduled ancient monument, to the proposed new Museum of Scotland, the Secretary of State refused consent on the advice of Historic Scotland for its removal to Edinburgh. For some time Historic Scotland had recognised that the cross needed to be taken under cover and had agreed with local parties that it ought to stay locally, but there was no consensus as to where this should be. In 1997 a compromise was struck. The Cross was placed in the ownership of Historic Scotland which has loaned it to the Museum of Scotland (Figure 3). Here it is being displayed for three years, most appositely, at the entrance to the *Kingdom of the Scots* gallery. Thereafter it will be accessible in a church in the care of Historic Scotland, 6 km away from its previous location, in an adjacent parish (see Conclusions, below).

Ownership of carved stones on ecclesiastical sites is historically more problematic. For example, some early medieval sculptures have been re-appropriated for more recent gravemarkers and present day ownership claimed by the families on whose plots the stones now lie. Further ambiguities can arise if the ownership of a church, churchyard or burial ground is not known. The Church of Scotland Property and Endowment Act 1925 passed ownership and responsibility for parish burial grounds from the heritors of parishes to parish councils, a responsibility later transferred to the local authorities. Property rights and responsibilities for parish churches and churchyards passed to the Church of Scotland Trustees. Since these transactions did not necessarily involve formal legal conveyance, it is sometimes difficult to get anyone to accept responsibility for a site that may

Figure 3 Stone conservators and archaeologists prepare the Dupplin Cross in advance of its removal to the Museum of Scotland. *Crown copyright Historic Scotland*

include early medieval material. Without a recognised owner it can be difficult for anyone to take necessary remedial action.

IMPLICATIONS

I will now turn to some of the planning, management, presentation and interpretation issues that can arise when trying to retain and convey an appropriate sense of relationship between a sculpture, its archaeological context and landscape setting.

Place
The reality, as we all know, is that sculpture continues to erode if exposed to the elements. At Dunadd (near Kilmartin, Argyll and Bute) in 1979 a cast of the carved, living rock was placed over the original to protect it from visitor traffic. But this is a rare example of early medieval rock art and simply covering up or reburying most early medieval sculptures is scarcely an option because they are vertical or too prominent above the ground.

For the monuments in its own care, Historic Scotland has adopted a range of conservation and presentation strategies. Some more durable sculptures, as at Kildalton (Islay, Argyll and Bute) are still in the open and are monitored regularly. At Fowlis Wester (Perthshire and Kinross) where the Pictish cross-slab was presumed not to be in its original location, the original was moved to the adjacent church and a replica placed on its site in 1991. The sculptures from Keills chapel (Argyll and Bute) were gathered together in the 1970s and placed in the chapel that was re-roofed for this purpose (Figure 4). This did involve moving a cross that was presumed to be in its original position but a simple outline marker replaced it. At Ardchattan (Argyll and Bute) shelters were erected in the late 1990s along wall-faces to provide protection for the most important medieval carved stones, including the early medieval cross-slab, and these have been moved there for this purpose.

Elsewhere, we have occasionally placed shelters directly over unmoved stones, whether they were still *in situ* or not, such as at Eassie (Angus) or Dunfallandy (Perth and Kinross). However, this was done nowhere more controversially than at Sueno's Stone (Moray). This sculpture is almost certainly in its original location, though re-erected.[15] Furthermore, due to its extreme tall and narrow dimensions – it stands 6.5 m high – any move was risky and we opted, after public consultation and an architectural design competition, to build a modern shelter over it. The condition of the sculpture and of the environment within the shelter is regularly monitored. At Aberlemno (Angus) there has been a lively debate with the local community for the last 30 years or so about whether it would be appropriate to relocate the four sculptures located here and where would be a suitable local venue. There has been public concern about the condition of the sculptures here

Figure 4   Keills chapel, re-roofed, with a simple stone outline marker indicating the prior location of the free-standing cross. *Crown copyright Historic Scotland*

since 1889 and the first designs for shelters over the sculptures date from 1913. However, this solution has continued to be rejected for a host of reasons, not least their juxtaposition with a busy roadside. Since the 1980s the carved stones have been wrapped in thermal material and boxed over winter to protect them from harmful cycles of freezing and thawing, as well as salt from the road. Angus Council is now taking the lead, in partnership with Historic Scotland, to see if funding can be secured for the development of a purpose-built shelter in the village. This initiative fits in with Angus Council's aim of creating and enhancing a formal network of 'satellite' sites from their Pictavia Visitor Centre. The future design and precise siting of this structure will no doubt excite much interest and debate, as it should. Only in the case of Sueno's Stone has a large-scale modern building been designed in Scotland to house early medieval sculpture and the design chosen has received criticism for missing the opportunity to include a public viewing platform. Its prominent architectural form has also elicited much comment – 'a giant packing case' – although it should be remembered that it is sited on the edge of a built up area and surrounded on two of its three sides by roads (Figure 5). Not surprisingly, the advisability of capturing stones in the environment of glass shelters also continues to be questioned by some conservation professionals as well as visitors who can be disappointed when sculpture cannot readily be photographed, for instance.

Historic Scotland's most common formula where the sculpture is not earthfast, or can be readily moved, has been to adopt and adapt existing, often historic, buildings to house it. Inevitably this sometimes places constraints on how the sculpture can then be displayed, but is the easiest means of ensuring continuity between findspot and sculpture and avoiding unnecessary new build on historic sites.

Other bodies have adopted broadly the same approach as Historic Scotland. For example, Perth Museum and Art Gallery brought the Crieff Burgh Cross into the basement of the former Tolbooth, now the local Tourist Information Centre.[16]

Dilemmas

But these interventionist strategies inevitably raise questions for which we must answer to future generations. It has been observed that the concept of conservation is regarded in international and national policies as a legal and moral ideal, a moral obligation on all human beings. As a result it is suggested that the surrendering of monuments to destruction has become no longer a question of interests but of morals. This raises the question of what we may be losing in our efforts to conserve sculpture. In taking our glass cases to the objects rather than vice versa is their loss of accessibility (e.g. for photography) and visual amenity acceptable? Is it really desirable to halt the ageing process? Does age not enhance beauty and value? What could be the unforeseen and undesirable consequences of our interventions? These are some of the many observations and questions raised by Walderhaug Sætersdal[17] in her critique of Norwegian rock art conservation.

For my part, there are two main issues that I think merit closer attention in Scotland. Firstly, any decisions as to the future of individual sculptures ought to include a review of the significance and value of its present location in relation to the national *corpus* as a whole. What is the point at which further relocation of material still *in situ* or associated with its findspot would be unacceptable? Would it not be desirable to ensure that a representative range of original material remains *in situ*? By representative I do not mean simply representative of monument type and art style, but also of geographical diversity, archaeological context and function. In exploring this issue I would like to see decisions informed by the merits of the sculpture rather than led by what may be the short-term desires and demands of others, such as problems with public access.

The second issue demanding attention leads on from this, namely whether it is acceptable to allow such sculpture to 'die'. There has been little recent debate on this in Scotland and certainly no official sanctioning of the idea. In this respect the symbolic or living religious significance of sculpture must not be forgotten. In 1959, the Reverend George MacLeod of the Iona

Figure 5 Sueno's Stone, illuminated at night. *Crown copyright Historic Scotland*

Community considered that the shattered remains of St John's Cross on Iona, should also be 'allowed to decay in the open in God's good time' – views which did not extend to the abbey buildings and were not shared by others (Figure 6). What, I wonder, would the original patrons and craftsmen have wished us to do? No individual or community, arguably not even the church, can truthfully claim a direct and continuous descent from these people, although their modern sense of affiliation and identity may be strong indeed. There is also the argument, because of this disjunction with past or living traditions, that we are 'no longer intimate enough with this legacy to rework it creatively'.[18]

Since the scanning technology now exists for accurate 3D record and replication without any of the adverse affects that go with the physical act of taking a cast, 'dying' is an option to which we should probably give more consideration. (Although it is not likely to be the popular choice and any such debate would bring to the fore the tension between the sculpture as 'art' and as 'monument'). Whether such replicas are displayed locally or in more distant museums is another question (they could be displayed in both!), but it would be true to say that museums do not tend to want to display replica material in their permanent displays. Yet, as we have seen at the 1999 Pictavia Visitor Centre (by Brechin, Angus), replica and reconstructed material can be imaginatively and effectively used to 'flesh out' what is otherwise only a small core of original material.

It should be noted, in passing, that living Christian religious values can work 'against' a sculpture that is perceived to be pagan. In 1977 the Kirk Session at Strathmiglo, having decided that the symbol-bearing boulder here was not of Christian origin, was not prepared to accept responsibility for its upkeep. As a result, when it was moved, it was to the entrance to the churchyard.

We should also not lose sight of the fact that weathering and erosion are far from being the only destructive forces we are dealing with, factors that may preclude preservation *in situ*: vandalism, pollution and agricultural activities are some of the more common problems.

Space
To quote the Venice Charter: 'A monument is inseparable from the history to which it bears witness and from the setting in which it occurs'.[19] In the first instance this means we should protect the archaeological site of which the sculpture is an integral part – a burial place, monastery or church, for instance. This can take the form of visible and invisible remains, undisturbed or otherwise. When their extent is known they can be legally protected through scheduling, or through the planning process.[20,21,22,23] But this supposes that we have recognised and understood the context and function of our sculpture and the nature and extent of such sites. Alas, this is very rarely the case. Exploration or modern archaeological excavation around *in situ* material has

Figure 6   St Martin's Cross and St John's Cross, in front of Iona Abbey. St John's is a concrete replica, the original being on display in the site museum. *Crown copyright Historic Scotland*

been limited to very few sites, and has rarely been extensive. Likewise, there has been little exploration of sites from which sculpture is known or presumed to have originated.

In terms of the historical and archaeological interests, it is also desirable to preserve their setting. This can perhaps be considered in terms of those qualities and features of the surrounding landscape that relate to and/or are critical to understanding and appreciating the monument. The ancient monuments legislation allows for the formal protection of land around a monument that is 'essential for the monument's support and preservation', but the extent of this is likely to be limited to a 'support zone' for measures, such as fencing, to protect the site.[24] The present legislation says nothing about amenity or setting, and for this we have to rely on planning mechanisms or agreements with landowners, etc. Nor are 'amenity' (*Concise Oxford Dictionary* 'pleasantness') or 'setting' clearly defined concepts in planning terms, and our tools for assessing either are rather underdeveloped for any sort of monument, let alone sculpture.[25] I know of only one instance, in 1947, of a formal consideration of how amenity in the context of a sculpture should be defined. A housing development was proposed around Sueno's Stone and the Ancient Monuments Board decided to object to any development within 50 feet of the monument.

The focus of protection in Europe has moved on since Pitt Rivers' day. During the nineteenth century museums were the focus of presentation and protection, but this developed at the end of the century to an interest in monuments as places, as I discussed earlier. Since the end of the Second World War, particularly in the last thirty years or so, there has been increasing recognition that monuments cannot be viewed in isolation, but as a part of a wider cultural landscape or historic environment.[26,27,28] It is in this environment that we now seek to preserve key features and qualities of the broader cultural landscape in which individual monuments operated, although it has to be noted that our legislation in Scotland does not tally with our present perceptions of the historic environment. To give an example, we have no knowledge of the immediate archaeological context of the roadside sculptures at Aberlemno, but we do believe that they were originally erected as markers along a prominent ridge forming a natural route of communication between the areas of modern Forfar and Brechin. It is important to ensure that we do not lose the ability to recognise this on the ground and for the sculpture to be able to tell its fullest story.

The implications of any development to protect sculpture must also be taken into the equation. Sometimes significant new buildings to house original material in its historic location are unavoidable, even at sensitive sites. Perhaps the most exciting form of purpose-built housing for sculpture I have seen is that constructed by Dúchas at Clonmacnoise in Ireland. But it should be noted that its construction adjacent to the early Christian monastery had to involve extensive archaeological excavation and the insertion of a modern building here was obviously controversial because of its impact on the setting of the site. It also succeeds in providing a secure, well-lit and beautifully laid out display space for the high crosses that were removed from the site for their safety and replaced with replicas.[29,30] Ideally we might have wished for more space above the crosses, but the potential height of the building was undoubtedly constrained by its sensitive location. Also, only a fraction of the Clonmacnoise assemblage, the largest in the British Isles at over 600, is able to be displayed.

To Tell a Story

Whether as scholars or tourists, we now want to actively experience the 'authentic' historic environment rather than observe from a safe distance.[31] Whether *in situ* or not, whether a reconstruction, replica or original, it is all the more incumbent on all of us dealing with the presentation and interpretation of these monuments to ensure that the story of their context is also told. Leaving to one side how we deal with the sculpture 'as art', the challenges include conveying a sense of the monumentality, original function and historic setting of this material. Fortunately, the tools at our disposal, particularly electronic media, are developing rapidly.

In part the task is about explaining the context of material, where this is known. One of the many strengths of the Tarbat Discovery Centre is that it conveys an understanding of the context of this material, as derived from the University of York's excavations of the presumed monastery. It is therefore about encouraging the visitor to look and think beyond the visitor centre or individual monument to the landscape around them. At St Vigeans, an eighth-to tenth century centre of secular, probably royal patronage, the visitor needs to be able to make the links beyond the cottage walls that a local benefactor donated to house the sculpture, to the prominent church mound where it was found, and beyond that to the related sites of early medieval southern Pictland (Figure 7).

Trails, such as Angus Council's *Pictish Trail*, a network of sites 'centred' on the Pictavia visitor centre, Highland Council's *Pictish Trail* or that in Aberdeenshire can also encourage visitors to make the physical and intellectual connection between such sites.

Where historical or other circumstances dictate that the sculpture is now distant, replicas or reconstructions can provide a powerful substitute on site (Figure 6). The issues in such instances include where on site these replicas should be located and, if including an element of reconstruction, what form this should take and how this should be self-documenting to present and future generations.

The Scottish Cultural Resources Access Network (SCRAN) is a vehicle for making catalogues of material, and so much more, available over the World Wide Web. We can now accurately replicate sculpture using non-invasive techniques, capture 3D models of the sculpture, reconstruct the monuments

Figure 7 The prominent church mound at St Vigeans from which a large collection of Pictish and Scottish sculpture was recovered in the nineteenth century. *Crown copyright Historic Scotland*

on the screen, examine them from all angles and even inspect them in a landscape. Stuart Jeffrey's PhD research at Glasgow University is an excellent example of what is possible. No sculpture need be inaccessible to those with access to a computer terminal, and there is the means to 'reconstruct' and 'replace' sculpture. A caution is needed however; as such approaches need to make it transparent and explicit at each stage how reliable the evidence is for what is shown.

CONCLUSIONS

Scottish early medieval sculpture is a cultural asset with largely untapped potential to celebrate Scotland's heritage in its full diversity, not least through the recognition of the diverse ethnic origins and international connections of its early medieval peoples. This is one of the ways in which this material has a particular relevance in terms of the *National Cultural Strategy*.[32] But attitudes to this material have changed dramatically over the 1000-plus years since it was created. Our present respect for this material was not shared throughout early medieval and medieval times, when political, social and economic causes led to much of it quickly losing its original function and being destroyed, buried or recycled.

What remains important today is that in all our actions, particularly those dealing with individual monuments in association with their findspots, we do not 'cultivate corners' and lose sight of the fact that early medieval sculpture is only a small corner of the 'great field' of Christian monuments.[33] We must also be conscious of the fact that by our actions we will be changing the historical significance of this material, potentially for political purposes, modelling the very past that we are seeking to protect. Whilst Pitt Rivers' policies on carved stones, effectively those we adopt today, are now reflected in international charters,[34] it could be said that our philosophical and ethical arguments in Scotland have not progressed far since his time. What has progressed over the last century is our conservation know-how, our recognition of the importance of setting and wider archaeological context, and the range of technological tools at our disposal.

In making decisions about the future of early medieval sculpture a critical understanding of the historical perspective, national overview, pragmatic approach and long term vision is desirable. On the one hand we need to understand why sculpture that has been moved has ended up where it has and what the legal and practical implications of this are. On the other hand, there is an increasing range of options available to us to seek to retain or replace the sculpture's sense of association with its place and setting. Our initial solutions may not be perfect, but nor need they be permanent. Because it is against the landowner's wishes the Dupplin Cross could not be retained *in situ*. Because there is no suitable location it cannot yet be returned to a suitable place within the same parish. Historic Scotland also acknowledges that the less local church in which it is being sited is not a perfect display space. In the short term its original site is to be commemorated with a modest marker, but a different owner may one day permit the erection of a replica. One day we may find a preferable local home for the original. It is by recognising that individual sculptures and their findspots still have a long history ahead of them that we can seek to reconcile the competing interests of the present, providing that today's actions remain reversible.[35]

References

1.   Foster, S.M., *Place, Space and Setting. The Future of Early Medieval Sculpture,* Groam House Museum, forthcoming.
2.   Breeze, D., 'Artefacts and monuments. The building blocks of identity', in Fladmark, J.M. (ed), *Heritage and Museums. Shaping National Identity,* Donhead 2000, pp. 183–9.
3.   Historic Scotland, *The Carved Stones of Scotland. A guide to helping in their protection,* Heritage Guide 2, 2001. Copies of this free leaflet are available from hs.conservation.bureau@scotland.gov.uk.
4.   Historic Scotland, 'Carved Stones: Historic Scotland's Policy', 1992, appendix in Maxwell, I., *The Preservation of Dark Age Sculpture,* 1994, and

in Bowman, E.O. and Robertson, N.M., (eds), *Stones, Symbols and Stories. Aspects of Pictish Studies. Proceedings from the Conferences for the Pictish Arts Society, 1992,* pp. 3–18.

5. Historic Scotland, *Ancient Monuments Board for Scotland. Forty-seventh Annual Report 2000,* The Stationery Office, 2001.

6. Anderson, J., 'Notes on the survival of pagan customs in Christian burial; with notices of certain conventional representations of "Daniel in the den of lions," and "Jonah and the 'whale,'" engraved on objects found in early Christian graves, and on the sculptured stones of Scotland, and crosses of Ireland', in *Proc Soc Antiq Scot,* Vol 11, 1876, pp. 363–406.

7. Anderson, J., *Scotland in Early Christian Times (Second Series). The Rhind Lectures in Archaeology for 1880,* David Douglas, 1881.

8. Pitt-Rivers, A.H., 'Paper on models of ancient monuments, and on some points in the development of the Celtic Cross in Scotland', in *Proc Soc Antiq London,* second series, Vol 13, 1891, pp. 174–81.

9. Pitt-Rivers, A.H., 'Typological museums, as exemplified by the Pitt-Rivers Museum at Oxford, and his provincial museum at Farnham, Dorset', in *J Soc Arts,* Vol 40, 1891, pp. 115–20.

10. Foster, S.M., *Place, Space and Setting. The Future of Early Medieval Sculpture,* Appendix, Groam House Museum, forthcoming.

11. Ibid.

12. Pitt-Rivers, A.H., 'Paper on models of ancient monuments, and on some points in the development of the Celtic Cross in Scotland', in *Proc Soc Antiq London,* second series, Vol 13, 1891, pp. 174–81.

13. Ancient Monuments And Archaeological Areas Act, 1979.

14. Scottish Executive, *Treasure Trove in Scotland. Information on Treasure Trove Procedures. Criteria for Allocation and the Allocation Process,* 2.2, 1999.

15. McCullagh, R.P.J., 'Excavations at Sueno's Stone, Forres, Moray' in *Proc Soc Antiq Scot ,* Vol 125, 1995, pp. 697–718.

16. Hall, M., et al, 'Of makings and meanings: towards a cultural biography of the Crieff Burgh Cross, Strathearn, Perthshire', in *Tayside Fife Archaeol J,* Vol 6, 2000, pp. 154–88.

17. Walderhaug Sætersdal, E.M., 'Ethics, politics and practices in rock art conservation', in *Public Archaeology ,* Vol 1, 2000, pp. 163–80.

18. Ibid, p. 176.

19. ICOMOS, *The 'Venice Charter',* 1964, article 6.

20. Scottish Office Environment Department, *National Planning Policy Guideline 5,* 1994.

21. Scottish Office Environment Department, *Planning Advice Note 42. Archaeology – the Planning Process and Scheduled Monument Consent Procedures,* 1994.

22. Scottish Office Development Department, *National Planning Policy Guideline 18,* 1998.

23. Historic Scotland, *Memorandum of Guidance on Listed Buildings and Conservation Areas,* 1998.

24. Ancient Monuments and Archaeological Areas Act, 1979, section 61(9).

25. Tyldesley, D., 'Landscape capacity study of the setting of the Heart of Neolithic Orkney World Heritage Site'. Paper submitted to *Conservation and Management of Archaeological Sites*, April 2001.

26. Saunders, A.D., 'A century of ancient monuments legislation 1882-1982', in *Antiq J*, Vol 63, 1983, pp. 11–33.

27. Kristiansen, K., 'The strength of the past and its great might'; an essay on the use of the past, in *J European Archaeology*,Vol 1, 1992, pp. 3–32.

28. Walderhaug Sætersdal, E.M., 'Ethics, politics and practices in rock art conservation', in *Public Archaeology,* Vol 1, 2000, pp. 163–80.

29. King, H., 'Moving crosses', in *Archaeology Ireland,*Vol 6:4, 1992, pp. 22–3.

30. Dúchas, *Clonmacnoise co. Offaly,* 1998.

31. Kristiansen, K., 'The strength of the past and its great might'; an essay on the use of the past, in *J European Archaeology,* Vol 1, 1992, p. 11.

32. Scottish Executive, *Creating our Future: minding our past, the national cultural strategy,* 2000.

33. Anderson, J., 'Notes on the survival of pagan customs in Christian burial; with notices of certain conventional representations of "Daniel in the den of lions," and "Jonah and the 'whale,'" engraved on objects found in early Christian graves, and on the sculptured stones of Scotland, and crosses of Ireland', in *Proc Soc Antiq Scot,* Vol 11, 1876, p. 365.

34. ICOMOS, *The Illustrated Burra Charter*, Australia ICOMOS, 1992, 42, 3 article 9.

35. An expanded version of this paper was presented as the Groam House Academic Lecture for 2001. This is published with full and detailed references, notes and acknowledgements as 'Foster, forthcoming'. Copies of this illustrated booklet are available from the Groam House Museum, High Street, Rosemarkie, IV10 8UF, Scotland, price £4.50 including p&p.

15

PHILOSOPHICAL NOTES ON THE PRACTICE OF CULTURAL HERITAGE CONSERVATION AND MANAGEMENT

Anne-Sophie Hygen

According to Aboriginal Australian belief all there is was created in *Dreamtime*, the unspecified and timeless past: language, song, dance, images, plants, animals, landscape formations and *Bininj Munggu*, which is the Aboriginals' term for themselves. According to some traditions, *Nayhyunggi* spirit beings created the world and gave the first people laws to live by. By other traditions, *The Rainbow Serpent* was the creator. The ancient laws regulate everything: how to live, social life, kinship systems and how to take care of the land. Generations after generations of young people are initiated into the Law.

Indigenous peoples had – and many still have – traditions connected to the care of their land: Aboriginal Australians, indigenous Americans, Saami peoples of the north and so on. Land and nature are not ours to exploit. Land is sacred and may be carefully harvested and managed, but not spoilt. In the Western European culture there is little left of this attitude to landscape. Ways of thinking which are self-evident to indigenous peoples are more or less foreign to us today. Presumably, however, this indigenous attitude was ours, too, some time in the maybe not so distant past.

In order to protect and manage the manifestations of the past we somehow need to recover forgotten knowledge, skills and attitudes. Still, I cannot but consider it culturally pathetic that we need to teach ourselves something that we used to take for granted and that some peoples still do.

The systems of economy and land use being as they are in the Western world, it is not very realistic even to hope that we can recover the 'original' prehistoric or historic landscapes. Since we have little collective methodological experience left, we cannot just 'go out and do it' anymore; when cultural heritage managers have tried to do just that, the results have usually not been very good. This means that practice alone is not sufficient in heritage management, we need thinking too. While there has been a theoretical surplus in archaeology and other cultural heritage sciences for the past several decades, in cultural heritage management there seems to have been a practical surplus combined with a considerable theoretical deficiency.

In cultural heritage management we need to know not only what to do but also the why and how of doing it. At hand to us are theories and models with which to create and implement methods. Based on theoretical thinking, methods for practising holistic attitudes to landscape and the elements in it are necessary to be able to handle past and present cultural phenomena. There are a number of relevant theories available to us if we do not have the time or the ability to develop them ourselves. Good instances are Pierre Bourdieu's theory of practice,[1] Anthony Giddens' theory of structuration,[2] the philosophical hermeneutics conveyed by philosophers such as Hans-Georg Gadamer[3] and Paul Ricoeur,[4] and the works of recent ecological philosophers.

But, of course, we cannot manage the cultural heritage with theories alone, to the same little extent as with practice alone. Theory without practice is just as meaningless as practice without theory. Practice has conscious as well as unconscious aspects, in much the same way as opinions and ideology – openly or camouflaged, directly or indirectly – are constituted in acts and expressions. The practical side of any theory should be emphasized and be active, causing reflection and practice to be tied together into a whole, as aspects of the same thing. This also means to appraise the practical side of theory as an activity producing knowledge.[5]

Spatial and contextual thinking has for the past few decades gradually been impacting upon archaeological thinking and interpretation. A very good example is Richard Bradley's study of British prehistoric rock carvings in the landscape from 1997.[6] The interpreted meaning of the images and symbols cannot be isolated to the images themselves or to the rock surfaces they were carved in. Of great importance are the rules and conventions behind the relationship between the distribution of different motifs in the landscape, how chosen rock surfaces are positioned and distributed in relation to local topography in the prehistoric landscape, and the context of other cultural remains.[7] Such analysis makes it possible to interpret human use of and movements in the landscape and possible communicative and identifying functions of the rock carvings[8] besides the ritual ones.

In cultural heritage, however, an area and an activity in which it would be fair to presume that contextual, recursive thinking was a matter of course, we have traditionally been considering each site and monument individually and in isolation. We have admired, studied, preserved and conserved monuments as 'object things', and often we still do.

According to this attitude, the bygone and its physical manifestations are out there, we think that we own them and can use and exploit them for whatever purposes – because they belong to us. We have seen plenty of sorry results of such attitudes in cultural heritage; I will restrict myself to mentioning ruthless economic over-exploitation of heritage sites connected to massive tourism. They become the objects – we become the sole subjects. However, disregarding the physical, spatial and mental contexts of which they are an obvious and integral part may well be regarded as a major violation of elementary ethical rules.

Consequently, in order to do our job properly we have to pose questions not only about the why and how of cultural heritage management, but also such as 'on behalf of whom do we protect, plan and manage the cultural heritage?'

The obvious answer to this question is, of course, that we do it for ourselves in the present – we simply like heritage sites and realise the necessity and importance of them. More nobly, we say we do it for future generations because we regard the cultural heritage as a collective value, which is not for us exclusively to own. It simply is not ours. Our job is to interpret the fragmented fragments of the past and manage them as a loan from future generations of 'mankind'.

But are the present and future perspectives sufficient? We should include the past peoples, too, in our considerations and dealings with the sites and monuments and their landscapes: the people who – individually and collectively – thought, created and used what for us constitutes the cultural heritage. How can we philosophically and practically overcome the time barriers between past, present and future in our dealings with past phenomena? How may we conquer the distance? We cannot ask them because they don't exist anymore. But we can act as if we could. The key word here is involvement.

For Martin Heidegger, involvement is what makes the difference between the ontical and the ontological viewpoint.[9] The ontical consideration represents a situation where subjects from a distance regard phenomena from their limited standing point – from the outside position – defining the phenomena through descriptive facts. The ontological consideration, however, represents a situation where subjects blend with the phenomena through involvement and acknowledgement of being as a basic, existential human state influencing the way phenomena are regarded. This is the human process implying the seeking to penetrate the surface of the phenomena and into the being of things. Heidegger calls this process of de-severance a human existential: procuring it, bringing it close, putting it in readiness, having it to hand, conquering the remoteness.[10,11,12]

Of course, we do have an ontical–ontological dilemma between past and present here, since neither the time gap nor the massive cultural differences are to be disregarded. A way out of this dilemma is to down-play the linear time structure and acknowledge a model which ties us all as human beings in the world to an alternative structure of time and space and to a human and action oriented community.[13]

In other words: bringing the bygone close to and within us through involvement and searching for understanding makes it possible to master it, take mental possession of it, make it our own and give it meaning; to make it real and existing by giving the phenomena mental space. Involvement with integrity, respect, insight, understanding, experience and acknowledgement is not only a challenge in heritage management but an ethical obligation.[14]

Even though we cannot ask 'them' about the right way to manage their landscapes and properties, we should act as if we could. Is it possible to go into prehistoric peoples' heads? Yes, archaeologists do it all the time, whether we realise it or not. In fact, we have to do it in order to be able to name and interpret past phenomena at all.[15] Furthermore, Joseph Campbell, American philosopher of religion and mythology, strongly questions whether modern man in fact differs fundamentally from prehistoric man. He says:

> You have got the same body, with the same organs and energies, that Cro Magnon man had thirty thousand years ago. Living a human life in New York city or living a human life in the caves, you go through the same stages of childhood, coming to sexual maturity, transformation of the dependency of childhood into the responsibility of manhood and womanhood, marriage, the failure of the body, gradual loss of its powers, and death. You have the same body, the same bodily experiences, and so you respond to the same images.[16]

The logic is that in a global perspective there are in principle many shared mythological and ritual patterns. Campbell's common denominator is the *archetype*. Archetypes may be regarded as manifestations of the organs of the body and their powers. Campbell says:

> The psyche is the inward experience of the human body, which is essentially the same in all human beings, with the same organs, the same instincts, the same impulses, the same conflicts, the same fears.[17]

Cultural differences evolve because the archetypes, 'the elementary ideas' in Jung's terms, appear in different costumes: 'The differences in the costumes are the results of environment and historical conditions'.[18]

Consequently, there are in principle two different ways to consider the past. We can emphasise the distance, the fundamental differences in adaption and cultural forms, or, we can emphasise the closeness, the fundamental sameness, by focusing the archetypical in what it is to be a human being.[19] This may also be illustrated by Heidegger's notion of 'the temporality of being human'; the past continues as a constant summing up of something which has been in something which is.[20] Existentially, this means to regard human beings as included and involved in a space of contextual time, rather than being at a certain point on a straight line within a linear time concept. Through involvement, pre-conditions are created for the human project of being, within a narrative whole – like the Aboriginal *Dreamtime*. Narratives, then, may be regarded as a space for ambiguity – for different, even opposing interpretations.

I think that our greatest barrier against this kind of thinking is the one-dimensional, linear and strictly chronological concept of time – or rather, that we think that the linear time concept is the only possible way of thinking about time. But we, too, operate with more cyclical and circular time concepts, and when we start thinking about it we easily find a number of good examples, in real life and in literature, of alternative and supplementing time conceptions. Any concept of time is a cultural phenomenon, and the linear concept is not even a very old one.

Obviously, we are very different from the peoples who created the monuments and sites which for us constitute the cultural heritage. Still, by realizing the inherent ambiguity, we may recognize a door which is slightly open to a non-possesive and non 'culture-imperialist' attitude to their manifestations, therefore to how to take care of them. In the perspective of today, this model involves not only the authorities and the people in charge of managing the cultural heritage, but the stake-holders at different levels too. This means that when we deal with cultural heritage sites and monuments through involvement into different cultural forms – past and present – we deal with them and us in a three-dimensional time-space-human being perspective. This attitude makes it possible to practice an ethic of cultural heritage planning, conservation and management.

Let us explore some examples of how we may apply this multi-dimensional attitude of involvement in practical conservation. My first example is the conservation of medieval masonry ruins based on the norm 'conserve as found'; the second, the ecological management of prehistoric rock art.

Before we decide to start conservation of a ruin, we have three choices[21] – and in this case, the ruin should be regarded as a miniature landscape. Choices, of course, are what planning is all about: making decisions which impact upon the future, sometimes with disastrous results and sometimes with quite good ones:

Should we leave it alone?
This is a rather selfish approach since we decide on behalf of future generations that they will be denied the monument. If we do nothing, deterioration will go on and the ruin will end up becoming a shapeless heap of rubble.

Should we restore?

Restoration is often based on speculation and fantasy and the motives may be other than saving the monument itself. Motives could be very suspect and have nothing to do with the ruin itself: such as religious, political and economic motives and one-dimensional tourism. Restoration often obscures the original monument and even destroys it forever. On the other hand, purposes like education and the raising of public awareness could, of course, be perfectly valid and honorable reasons for restoration if performed with sensitivity and care.

Should we conserve?

Much can be done by good documentation, management and monitoring of the site. When conservation is necessary it should be done with respect for all original material. This means the minimum of intervention with the maximum of quality in technique and materials. Even if conservation often means the introduction of some new material, there must be a balance between the need to preserve and a determination not to alter the appearance. Which means – to the largest possible extent – conserve as found.

The good thing about this principle is that it may easily be applied in practice. It is done by studying and understanding the structure of the remains of the building and by creating the conservation strategy accordingly. Understand the structure – that principle applies for small as well as for large scale planning; understand the structure and be as true to it as possible. The rubble in a double skin corework wall should be conserved as rubble, and the ashlar as ashlar, without trying to change the visual appearance or using different materials. This means, for instance, the use of mortar no harder than the original bedding mortar. Which also means, of course, that the use of concrete should be banned for all times.

A good example of a ruin preserved as found is Wigmore Castle in Herefordshire. Wigmore Castle was untouched and unspoilt before conservation and had survived as a virtually 'undiscovered romantic ruin'. But there were serious fears that the ruin would completely collapse. Little of the plaster survived, the masonry had eroded, stone-robbing had left the corework exposed, the ruin was overgrown with trees and plants and the broken wall-tops were overgrown with a dense though protective mat of vegetation.[22]

The challenge was to find a conservation method which would minimise intervention and preserve the appearance while at the same time ensuring the structural stability and safe access to visitors. Since the site was unaffected by previous and intrusive repairs they had the unique opportunity to create and apply a sound conservation philosophy, based on the natural mechanisms which had stabilized and preserved the castle ruins in its natural context. The chosen principle which was practiced was preserve as found. Thereby, English Heritage adopted a pioneering approach to conservation, as opposed

178

to the twentieth century main principle 'arrest the decay and freeze the masonry', which included removal of all vegetation and covering the broken wall tops with concrete. They restored Wigmore Castle as found, leaving it as a romantic ruin.[23] By applying a holistic and ecological view of the natural and cultural environment, the castle ruin was returned to its verdant state.[24,25]

We will continue the ecological thinking into the next example – ecological management of prehistoric rock art sites and environments, and consider this example, too, as a metaphor for the larger landscape.

At the Archaeological Museum in Stavanger in south-east Norway they have developed an ecological management philosophy that they apply in practice in a very constructive way. One of the great challenges of preservation of rock art sites is the growth of lichen, moss, and all kinds of high and low-growing vegetation. They have formulated problems like:[26]

- Trim a tree and it grows with double speed next year.
- Cut a tree down and five ones new grow up.
- Rotting twigs and roots add to the growth in the area.
- Spraying with biocides disturbs the established vegetation balance and may stimulate growth of new and unwanted species.

They have developed some very simple and sensible ecological advice for how to deal with vegetation based on the fact that an intrusion into nature always leads to secondary effects:[27]

- Trim trees regularly, not as an all-out effort.
- Trim both twigs and roots, this will reduce growth.
- Removing low-growing branches may be better than cutting the tree, this will provide sufficient light and air.
- Immediate removal of piles of twigs and leaves prevents natural manuring close to the site.
- Encourage the development of frugal species of herbs and grass in natural environments.

They sum this philosophy up in a few punch-lines, with the common heading *'play on nature's team'*:[28]

- Remember the environment around the site. A well-managed area inspires greater respect for the heritage site, gives better distribution of wear and a better total experience of the site.
- Don't regard nature as your enemy, chose your plant friends with care. Encourage the growth of friendly species.
- Don't just do management work when the weather is good. Plant materials are often more manageable during the rain.

- Use the different seasons well. Vegetation care in autumn, leaves the site nice and tidy in spring when visitors start coming in.
- Visit the site as if you are an ordinary tourist and observe how the visitors behave. You will see the site with different eyes and get good management ideas.

One practical example of this kind of thinking is to open up sites to light and air instead of fighting algae, lichens and moss directly on the carved surfaces, which may do a lot of harm. By careful and basically non-intrusive measures we may simply change the living conditions for unwanted species and encourage wanted ones. Another example is to plant local sticky bushes where we do not want visitors to walk. By very simple ecological measures we may steer the development in the direction we want. The very satisfactory result of this technique is that when the archaeologists and botanists have finished their environmentally friendly work on the sites, you can hardly notice that they have been there at all.[29]

The philosophy of minimum intrusion and conserve as found, combined with an environmental thinking in conservation, preservation and management practice fullfills, in my opinion, our ethical obligations within a holistic past-present-future perspective. Furthermore, it satisfies the preconditions of ontological involvement in the pragmatic reality. By involvement, we may penetrate the surface of phenomena into the being of things: into the structure of ruins – the shadows of buildings that were once thought, built and meant in a specific way; into the rock carvings in their cultural, ritual and natural landscapes; and into the prehistoric and historic landscapes at large.

We are very much closer to acting as if we could ask our own indigenous peoples how we should deal with their surviving material culture in the landscape but I think it will be impossible to include this in practical conservation. By the application of this kind of ethical conservation philosophy in planning and practice, I think we have a fair chance of avoiding the most terrible mistakes.

However, not only should we try to act as if we could ask practical advice of our own indigenous peoples. We can, too, learn from indigenous peoples of today, for instance from Australian Aborigines to whom landscape, tradition, rock art, body painting, song and music, dance, stories, social rules and identity cannot in any way be divided. We can listen to people like Stuart Oliver of the *Altyerre* people, an Aboriginal elder and owner of a rock art site at Ewaninga near Alice Springs, who says on an information board by a major rock carving site:

My father and my grandfather used to tell me all about what I can do. They used to teach me… I might pass away and you gotta hang on, you too, keep goin', keep going look after place. Don't leave it.

180

References

1. Bourdieu, P., *Outline of a Theory of Practice*, Cambridge Studies in Social Anthropology, Cambridge University Press, 1977.
2. Giddens, A., *The Constitution of Society. Outline of the Theory of Structuration*, Polity Press, 1984.
3. Gadamer, H-G., *Truth and Method*, second revised edition, Sheed & Ward, 1993.
4. Ricoeur, P., *Hermeneutics and the human sciences*, Maison des Sciences de l'Homme and Cambridge University Press, 1981.
5. Bourdieu, P. and Waquant, L.J.D., *Den kritiske ettertanke. Grunnlaget for samfunnsanalyse. Det Norske Samlaget* (original title: *Réponses. Pour une anthropologie réflexive*, 1991), 1993, pp. 41–42.
6. Bradley, R., *Rock Art and the Prehistory of Atlantic Europe. Signing the Land*, Routledge, 1997, pp. 8–16.
7. Ibid., pp. 8–16.
8. Ibid., pp. 78, 88–89.
9. Heidegger, M., *Being and Time*, Blackwell, 1962.
10. Ibid., pp. 22, 31, 117–18, 121, 132–33, 139–40.
11. von Wright, G.H., *Myten om fremskrittet. Tanker 1987-1992 med en intellektuell selvbiografi*, Cappelens upopulære skrifter, 1994, p. 132.
12. Hygen, A-S., *Fornminneforvaltning i praksis. Vern, bevaring og bruk av førreformatoriske kulturminner* [English summary pp. 121–34: *Prehistoric heritage management in practice. Protection, preservation and use of prehistoric sites and monuments.*], Arkeologiske avhandlinger og rapporter fra Universitetet i Bergen, 1999, pp. 41, 127.
13. Ibid., pp. 50, 129.
14. Ibid., pp. 40, 127.
15. Hodder, I., *Theory and Practice in Archaeology*, Routledge, 1996, p. 16.
16. Campbell, J. [with B. Moyers], *The Power of Myth*, Doubleday, 1988, p. 37.
17. Ibid., p. 51.
18. Ibid., pp. 51–52.
19. Hygen, A-S., *Fornminneforvaltning i praksis. Vern, bevaring og bruk av førreformatoriske kulturminner.* [English summary pp. 121–134: *Prehistoric heritage management in practice. Protection, preservation and use of prehistoric sites and monuments.*] Arkeologiske avhandlinger og rapporter fra Universitetet i Bergen, 1999, pp. 37, 126.
20. Heidegger, M., *Being and Time*, Blackwell, 1999, pp. 382ff.
21. Course in the conservation of masonry ruins, West Dean College, 20–23. February 2001. The practical consequences of such ethical principles – such as 'conserve as found' – in relation to masonry ruins are described and discussed by Ashurst in several publications, for instance in Ashurst, J. and Dimes, F.G., *Conservation of Building and Decorative Stone.* Vol. 1 and 2, Butterworth–Heinemann, 1990. The notion of 'conserve as found' connected to ruins is also discussed by Greenhow, I., *Beyond Repair. Radical Approaches to the Conservation of Ruins*, Dissertation for the degree of Master

of Science in Historic Conservation, Oxford Brooks University School of Planning and University of Oxford Department of Continuing Education, 2000, pp. 23–25.

22.	Greenhow, I., *Beyond Repair. Radical Approaches to the Preservation of Ruins,* Dissertation for the degree of Master of Science in Historic Conservation, Oxford Brooks University School of Planning and University of Oxford Department of Continuing Education, 2000, pp. 23-25.

23.	Ibid., p. 26.

24.	Ibid., pp. 29–30.

25.	See also the response to a letter to the Editor by Glyn Coppack in *Current Archaeology*, No 168, Vol XIV No 12, May 2000, p. 484.

26.	Bakkevig, S., 'Noen praktiske erfaringer og råd om skjøtsel på helleristningefelt', in Høgestøl, M. et al, *Helleristningsfeltene på Austre Åmøy, Stavanger kommune, Rogaland.* Dokumentasjon, sikring og tilrettelegging av feltene I til VI–5. AmS–Rapport 9, 95–99, 1999, p. 97.

27.	Ibid.

28.	Ibid., pp. 97–99.

29.	Bakke, B. et al, 'Bergkunst i Rogaland', in Hygen, A-S. (ed), *Fire år med Bergkunstprosjektet 1996-1999. Riksantikvarens Bergkunstprosjekt Sikring av Bergkunst 1996–2005,* Riksantikvarens rapporter nr. 29–2000, 107–131, Riksantiksvaren, 2000, pp. 117–20.

Further Reading

Ashurst, J. and Dimes, F.G., *Conservation of Building and Decorative Stone.* Vols 1 and 2, Butterworth–Heinemann, 1990.

16

THE CONTRIBUTION OF PROFESSIONAL ENGINEERS TO THE CONSERVATION OF THE HISTORIC LANDSCAPE

Geoffrey Clifton

I am a professional engineer with a passion for historic buildings, who is frequently involved in developments in historic cities. I have worked on many old buildings, two of which in particular give me great pleasure. They are two of our greatest medieval cathedrals – Wells and Lincoln, the second of which is very much in the area covered by this conference. I am a strong believer in the need for professionals to cross boundaries and to become involved in parallel professions in order to serve the needs of the community and our clients. Whilst working closely with architects and planners, it is with archaeologists that I have seen the need to become more involved. This has resulted in Gifford and Partners having a large archaeological team as part of our engineering consultancy.

As an engineer how did I get involved in archaeology? I was the structural engineer for city centre developments in London, Chester and York, all of which have considerable historic remains below ground. These always caused problems in finding the right solution for foundations, service trenches, drainage and there was often a lack of understanding between engineers, clients and archaeologists. This frequently created difficulties such as delays and changes to schemes. Then, whilst working on the Chester City Walls project, I found an archaeologist who understood the principles of engineering and business priorities as well as being renowned in his own profession.

Suddenly it was possible to talk as a team without conflicts and with trust to clients, regulatory authorities, etc. and to find solutions that suited everybody. Yes, our priorities were all different but they could be reconciled to everyone's advantage. Problems became opportunities. It as at this point that we set up the archaeological section in our practice and began to integrate engineers and archaeologists.

A few case studies will illustrate the contributions that we can make

CHESTER CITY WALLS

Chester still has a complete circuit of the City walls, two sides of which are on the line of the original Roman fort and incorporate much original Roman masonry, with the other two being on the line of the Saxon extensions (Figure 1).

Over the years the walls have been modified, partly as they deteriorated, but also in response to changing political circumstances, for example: the refortification in the civil war, the transformation into wall walks in the period of Queen Anne, and the Victorian restorations. In the 1960s some interventions were needed particularly to the East Wall, as it was rotating out of plumb. The wall was grouted, but by the 1980s monitoring of the walls was showing significant signs of movement particularly in the two sides on the line of the original Roman walls. Gifford was appointed to advise on what to do before they fell over, as by then the rotation was evident and the wall was also beginning to split (Figure 2).

A non-invasive investigation was started that involved engineers and archaeologists working out the history of the wall together in both archaeological and engineering terms, each discipline adding considerably to the other's understanding of the process. Whilst the results of this investigation gave us much presumed information, little hard evidence of the internal construction of the wall was available and radar surveys or mini borings could add little of value. A joint approach was made to the Royal Commission and English Heritage explaining the need to fully understand the composition of the walls in order to properly stabilise them. Any scheme based on inadequate information would suffer the same fate as previous attempts, which had often made matters worse. The investigation would have to be sufficient to understand the wall's history, its construction and strength. It would then be possible to decide on what to do. The only appropriate investigation that would yield sufficient information was to take slices down through the wall to foundation level.

A section through the wall was then archaeologically dismantled and the structure and history of the wall was analysed. Figure 3 shows a simplified structural history of the wall and Figure 4 shows its present complex form. This figure is a simplified version of the reality arrived at by careful interpretation.

The section was fascinating with all of the stages of the wall's history laid bare from the initial Roman turf rampart to the latest grouting exercise. Looking at the rampart one could still identify the outline of the turfs and it

Figure 1 Plan of the City Walls, Chester.

Figure 2 General view of the North Wall.

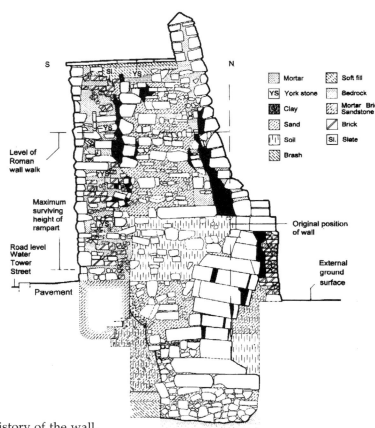

S   N

	Mortar		Soft fill
YS	York stone		Bedrock
	Clay		Mortar Brick Sandstone
	Sand		Brick
	Soil	Sl.	Slate
	Brash		

Level of Roman wall walk

Maximum surviving height of rampart

Road level Water Tower Street

Pavement

Original position of wall

External ground surface

Figure 3 History of the wall.

186

Figure 4 Present complex form.

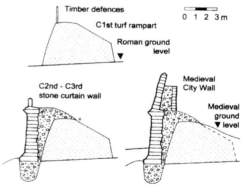

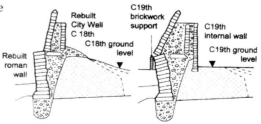

Figure 5 Section through the turf rampart.

187

was clear that the turfs were laid alternately upside down, so grass was to grass with some wood between. This is a very appropriate form of reinforced soil using the material as available to its best capability. I've used similar designs today, but I use geotextile rather than grass and withies (Figure 5).

The engineering calculations of the possible settlement of the rampart over time due to the loadings as the wall was modified and walkways added and the changes due to the cutting away of the rear of the rampart for barrack blocks showed a surprising correlation with the probable changes to the profile of the wall. It all served to give confidence in the archaeological results and in the engineering solutions.

A key point was that the investigation was neither an archaeological dig nor an engineering investigation but a combination of the two, as was the arrival at the understanding of the wall and of the solution to the instability.

A point, which caused much discussion, was how to reconstruct the wall. To rebuild it exactly as dismantled would merely result in it continuing to be unstable. It could be superficially reconstructed in the same way as it had been, out of plumb but with internal stiffening. Alternatively it could be reconstructed as it was at some previous time in history or with all the historical changes up to the present, but with the major bulges and leans removed. It was decided to rebuild the wall as it presently was but vertical and with some geotextile as a soft tie across the wall.

The investigation resulted in huge amounts of new information being discovered about the wall, which was of enormous benefit to the understanding of the wall. This has been written up in a book.[1] The main purpose of the exercise was achieved which was to stabilise the wall so that it is now set for another 2000 years.

VILLA DIONYSUS, CRETE

This project is well outside the study area but it is a useful example.

It is a Roman villa just outside Knossos. Much of the Roman remains in this area were dug through by Arthur Evans in his search for Minoan remains, but this villa survived (Figure 6). The villa has wonderful mosaics but at the time of our investigation it was sadly neglected with trees beginning to grow up through the mosaics (Figure 7). The British Archaeological School in Athens had a possible source of funding from an individual, to preserve the mosaics and display the villa in some way. Gifford were asked to visit, make an assessment and propose some costed solutions.

I visited the site with Tim Strickland, our Director of Archaeology, who is a well-known Romanist. We carried out a detailed desk study followed by a week on site researching the remains. Again the combination of engineering and archaeology brought wider understanding due to approaching what can be seen from different viewpoints. Trying to determine how the building

Figure 6 Villa Dionysus.

Figure 7 Mosaic floor.

189

Figure 8 Medieval Southampton.

Figure 9 General view of the site.

would have worked, with an engineer working from the drainage and foundations and an archaeologist using all the information to hand, plus historical researches, led to some lively debates, with a greater tendency to challenge received wisdom.

We produced a good understanding of the building and with our combined knowledge produced three options for its preservation and display: stabilisation of what was there; stabilisation with protection and full interpretation; and stabilisation with reconstruction of the possible villa for full interpretation. The third received much support, which I doubt it would have in the United Kingdom. But sadly one of the world recessions had an affect on the wealthy individual who was to have provided the funds and nothing came of the project.

This project reinforced my belief in the synergy of different disciplines coming together to produce real and timely answers.

WINKLE STREET, SOUTHAMPTON

Winkle Street is a site just within the line of the medieval City Walls still owned by Queens College, Oxford, to whom it has belonged since the thirteenth century. Historically the site contained a church and a hospital plus sundry buildings for the masters and governors of the hospital (Figure 8). By the nineteenth century it was largely covered with houses and small industrial buildings. Some of the Victorian house cellars had destroyed parts of the thirteenth century remains. The site was bombed during the Second World War and most of it was left derelict apart from a few garages and workshops. The site was cleared in the 1960s ready for development and used temporarily as a car park (Figure 9). At this point the archaeological implications became apparent and some exploratory excavations were made. It became clear that the site had much medieval archaeology remaining and as such no developer was interested in it. Excavations took place in 1968, 1984 and 1993 but on each occasion the developers were discouraged by the risk of the archaeology on the site.

It is exactly this sort of site that we relish, where by combining the skills of archaeology and engineering we can find a solution to a problem that has blighted the site for decades.

Due to its good location within the city, Winkle Street is a suitable site for high quality flats for affluent single city dwellers. We were asked to investigate the potential of the site by a housing developer. The existing information on the site was assembled and the archaeology ranked in order of importance and also in depth from the surface (Figure 10). An ultra light building, with minimum depth foundations sitting on top of piles, was then planned to fit onto the site. The probable pile positions were then plotted against the

191

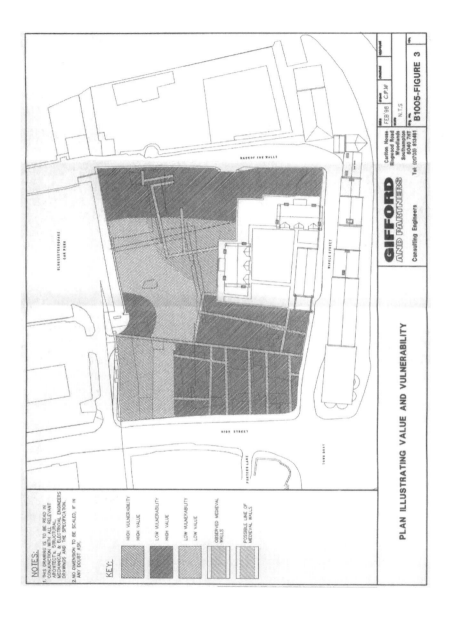

Figure 10 Plan of value and vulnerability, Winkle Street, Southampton.

192

Figure 11   Piling rig on site, Winkle Street, Southampton.

important archaeology on the site, and the building and pile foundations manoeuvred to avoid key areas.

The cellars and their floors were excavated and fully recorded and the medieval vaults and other remains were left *in situ*. The next task was to set out the locations of the piles on the ground and each location was probed. If any obstruction was encountered then the pile was either moved to a different location or the position excavated and recorded (Figure 11). In this way most of the archaeology on the site was left undisturbed. The drainage and incoming services routes were then designed in a similar fashion to keep them as high as possible and away from the more sensitive areas. The archaeologists then maintained a watching brief over all trench excavations, and routes were modified or excavation and recording of the archaeology took place as appropriate (Figure 12).

In this way it was possible to develop the site at a cost that was commercially viable, without compromising the history of the city.

HADRIAN'S WALL

Albemarle Barracks is an army base close to the Wall, which is accessed by means of a road built on top of the line of the Wall. The traffic to the base

Figure 12 Watching brief on the foundation excavations for a boundary wall, Winkle Street, Southampton.

may be increasing and may involve more tracked vehicles, so there is concern that the remains of the Wall may be damaged by the traffic. What should be done? Again the combination of engineering and archaeology means that a minimalist intervention can be planned that will provide us with the necessary information to assess the state of the archaeology and the affect of the traffic loads on the remains, and to quantify any risk.

CHEPHREN'S PYRAMID, GHIZA

This project started with a call from the Director of Antiquities in Cairo wanting us to send someone to Egypt urgently, as a pyramid was collapsing (Figure 13). After verifying that it was a genuine call and that the matter was urgent, someone was hastily despatched to Egypt. It transpired that an authorised excavation was proceeding into the Pyramid when stones from above the shaft began to fall progressively. What had been an authorised excavation hastily became unauthorised and external advice was required to sort it out or take the blame if all else failed! (Figure 14). An engineer obviously fitted that requirement. Fortunately we proposed a straightforward solution to the difficulty that repaired the damage, and all was well. The tunnel was once again authorised!

This shows an interesting example of the delicate balance between approval authorities and those who carry out investigations.

COMPTON VERNEY

Compton Verney is a Thomas Adam mansion house set within a Capability Brown historic landscape (Figure 15). The house had stood empty for fifty years, since it was vacated by the War Office at the end of the Second World War. Scheme after scheme was prepared for its re-use ranging from golf clubs to opera houses, but all failed before any work was done. Meanwhile the house was deteriorating at an increasing rate, much to the consternation of English Heritage, local planners, heritage groups, etc. In the end a scheme for building housing in the walled garden and converting the coach house into flats was approved, with the proviso that emergency repairs to the main house were carried out in order to stop the decay. At that point it was intended to refurbish the building as an hotel. But once the more profitable part of the work had been done, that is the housing elements, as well as the essential repairs to the house, which were a condition of the planning consent, nothing further happened, and the cycle looked in danger of happening again. At this point a wealthy benefactor decided that the house would make an excellent art gallery, provided that he could build a modern attachment for a fully climate-controlled gallery for visiting exhibitions.

Figure 13 Chephren's pyramid.

Figure 14 Tunnel excavation.

Figure 15 The Mansion House, Compton Verney.

Figure 16 The New Gallery extension, Compton Verney.

My role as an engineer was initially to assess the state of the building and to give an indication as to what was possible in terms of conversion both from a technical and a conservation point of view. I had two days to put together a costed report that could not have too many caveats.

The client having decided to go ahead, a full design team was appointed to prepare proposals for the house and landscape. A most interesting period of planning and negotiation then ensued to arrive at a scheme that met the needs and budget of the client, whilst meeting the conservation requirements of the various statutory bodies. The existing building was to be refurbished largely as originally designed with some areas converted to offices, and modern heating, lighting and other services installed. The finishes were to be kept simple and bland to suit an art gallery. These negotiations were reasonably straightforward; it was more difficult to get the agreement for the adjacent and integral modern gallery (Figure 16).

However the planners and statutory bodies were very aware that this was probably the last opportunity that this building had to be brought back into such appropriate use, and did not want to be too obstructive. Agreement was reached after much debate.

The historic landscape of the parkland was very much part of the discussion and agreement, and it is now being renovated and used as a sculpture park.

CONCLUSION

I am a great believer in different professions working closely together with plenty of overlap. It is often found that we are using similar skills and knowledge bases but starting from different positions and using different methods of analysis. We can learn much from each other. This is usually to the benefit of our clients and to society at large.

It is particularly true of the investigation of historic buildings and landscape where the interaction of engineers, geologists, archaeologists, environmentalists and other specialists can bring new and better understanding of the past and therefore crucially of what we should do for the future.

References

1.   LeQuesne, C., *Excavations at Chester – The Roman and Later Defences Part 1*, Chester City Council Cultural Services, 1999.

17

RECOMMENDATIONS ARISING FROM THE HISTORIC ENVIRONMENTS OF THE NORTH SEA REGION CONFERENCE 29–31 MARCH 2001

During the conference, a set of recommendations was produced by the delegates for future work on spatial planning and the historic environment:

OPENING STATEMENT

The historic environment is important:

- as a cultural asset in its own right
- as an educational and scientific resource
- in developing a sense of identity and pride of place
- as a means of recognising cultural diversity and yet drawing communities together in common action
- as a tool for regeneration and as an economic driver.

In all of this it is important that the principles of sustainability are applied and the asset is not compromised. Within Europe the value of the historic environment is recognised in policy frameworks such as the European Union's Spatial Development Perspective and the Council of Europe's Conventions on the Protection of the Architectural Heritage of Europe (Granada Convention, 1985), on the Protection of the Archaeological Heritage (revised) (Valetta, 1992), and on Landscapes (Florence, 2000). In developing co-operation within the Interreg North Sea Region it is essential that the need to identify, conserve, manage, enhance and promote the rich heritage of the area, and the potential benefits from so doing, are fully recognised both generally and through the instruments of spatial planning.

In particular we would like to propose the following recommendations:

1. The intergration of spatial planning into all levels of government

Archaeology and the protection and sustainable use of the historic environment as a whole should be an integral part of an holistic approach to spatial planning at all levels of government within each country.

National standards for an holistic approach to the conservation of the historic environment (including the protection of archaeological resources) should be established in each country, where possible, in accordance with international standards for spatial planning.

It is essential that archaeology is seen as an integral part of the planning process. Planners and archaeologists should work together with specialists.

2. To encourage governments to produce their own standards concerning the historic environment and to adopt existing european standards

Europe-wide standards and conventions exist already. It is important to raise awareness of these standards and conventions. Governments should be encouraged to ratify the Council of Europe Conventions on the Protection of the Architectural Heritage of Europe (Granada Convention, 1985), on the Protection of the Archaeological Heritage (revised) (Valetta, 1992) and on Landscapes (Florence, 2000) and to integrate their provisions into local, regional and national systems for the protection and sustainable use of the historic environment, including its archaeological resources.

Each country should also be encouraged to produce their own standards for the protection and sustainable use of the historic environment. These documents should be based on international statements of best practice such as the ICMOS Charters.

3. To encourage public involvement in archaeology and cultural heritage

Public access and social inclusion, which cannot be compartmentalised, should be built into all aspects of the planning process. Public awareness of the significance and relevance of the historic environment should be raised by projects to involve and engage them. The projects should be appropriate to the particular circumstances of the country concerned. Increased public awareness of the cultural heritage will help to protect it.

We should appreciate people's knowledge about a subject and their love for a place. A closer relationship with education and public awareness programmes will ensure future support by the general public for the preservation of significant elements of the historic environment.

4. To raise awareness of the importance of the historic landscape

The public perception of the historic environment, which is seen as point rather than area specific, needs to be changed. Currently, the natural environment has more emotive power than the historic environment. The landscape of Europe is the product of mankind's interaction with nature over a period of many millennia, and it is vital that the historic component of the landscape is fully recognised by all concerned.

All aspects of environmental protection and the management of the landscape should be approached in an integrated manner. It is important to acknowledge the multiple values of the landscape which include archaeological, ecological and mythological factors.

5. To encourage the integration of research into spatial planning development schemes

It is important to integrate cultural heritage and spatial planning in an effective partnership. More integrated approaches to archaeological investigation are being developed which include a strong research component. This integrated approach should be extended to include the allied professions routinely encountered by archaeologists, including spatial planning, landscape architecture and architecture. Thus research should also become an integral part of spatial planning development schemes.

6. The management of change

The physical evidence of the past should be understood as fully as possible in order to manage change sustainably.

Change is inevitable and desirable to meet the developing needs of society, but must be carried out in a way which protects significant elements of the historic environment.

7. To improve communication between different disciplines

All authorities should encourage co-operation and mutual exchange of views between the professions involved in the management of the historic environment.

As one of the principal professions involved in the management, archaeologists should develop closer co-operation and mutual   exchange of views with other concerned professionals locally, regionally, nationally and internationally.

ABSTRACTS OF UNPUBLISHED PAPERS

DILEMMAS IN CULTURAL TOURISM

Prof Magnus Fladmark, Robert Gordon University, Aberdeen
and Thor Heyerdahl Institute, Norway

The start of modern tourism in Europe and its different cultural elements
over time. From the age of pilgrimage to the present day. History as a source
of enrichment, pride, nationalism or shame. Stereotypes as friend or foe.
Heritage of resonance and dissonance, and historical interpretation in a
multicultural society. The case for a comprehensive framework for historical
interpretation to provide the context for strategic governance, custody,
presentation and accessing historical assets. Heritage assets in the branding
and marketing of nations, regions, places and organisations. 'Northlands
Heritage', or the potential for joint marketing by the countries around the
North Sea. The need for closer collaboration and strategic integration between
the tourism industry and cultural organisations. High culture and folk culture,
and the culture of enterprise and industry. The future of major shrines and
icons. Keepers without ears, products without appeal and markets ignored.
Future role of the state, subsidy junkies, philanthropists, volunteers and social
inclusion. Environmental planning, architects and cultural Philistines.
Protection, conservation and the Taliban. Cultural content, substance,
modernity and fashion. The consequence of thinking globally and acting
locally.

CULTURAL TOURISM AND THE ISLE OF MAN

Dr Andrew Foxon, Head of Professional Services, Manx
National Heritage, Isle of Man

The Isle of Man lies in the North of the Irish Sea and has its own distinct
history and traditions. Over thousands of years the changing Island

community has used the natural resources of the Island and its routes of communication to develop local economies tied into those of the neighbouring lands and trading partners.

The landscapes of the Isle of Man contain remains of these past activities. In a fast changing and growing economy, based on the finance sector and e-business, the natural and cultural resource in those landscapes has been recognised as precious to the community and worthy of protection and presentation.

This paper explores some of the economic and social issues within the Isle of Man, their impact on planning for the historic landscape (in its broadest sense) and the role played by the Island's integrated heritage service – Manx National Heritage. It focuses on the over-arching strategy for protection and interpretation represented by 'The Story of Mann' which views the whole of the Island as the resource, rather than elements within it. The impact of this approach on the role and development which cultural tourism plays on the Island is discussed.

ARCHAEOLOGY AS AN INSPIRATION FOR URBAN DEVELOPMENTS

Case studies: Leeuwarden and Weiwerd
Jan de Jong, Rijksdienst voor het Oudheidkundig Bodemonderzoek, Co-ordinator North, The Netherlands

The preservation of archaeological values has its legal base in the Monuments law and in several planning instruments. Besides that, inspiration and a creative approach to the chances archaeology offers for spatial designs are of the highest importance. This statement is illustrated by two cases. First the city of Leeuwarden where a large urban development threatens to damage several sites. Prospection and valuation of the sites leads to substantial changes in the design. The archaeological importance of the area has further been acknowledged when the construction of a national route resulted in well preserved mesolithic and Roman sites. The ROB was a partner in the discussion with the city and the ministry of traffic.

The second case is Weiwerd, a dwelling mound near the port of Delfzijl. Due to industrial activity 80% of the houses and farms were abandoned and demolished. Until recently the plans of Seaport Delfzijl intended to demolish all the buildings and to incorporate the mound in the industrial area. A private organisation started a campaign to secure the future of the historic buildings and the archaeological values. Now a development scheme has been prepared in which new architectural qualities, the quality of the existing buildings and the archaeological and landscape qualities are significant features in the process.

CONSERVATION PLANNING AND THE HISTORIC ENVIRONMENT
Royal Clarence VictuallingYard, Gosport
Dr Gerald Wait, Gifford and Partners Ltd, Southampton, United Kingdom

Over the past five years the Conservation Management Plan has become the tool of choice of the conservation movement in the UK. With its emphasis on a holistic approach (first pioneered by James Semple Kerr in Australia) the methodology is ideally suited to the large, mult-facetted sites of historic interest that are increasingly being drawn into the arena of regeneration.
Conservation plans have been most frequently created by, and for, conservation agencies of various national and regional governments. However, what happens when a site of great historic importance is also key to regeneration of an under-developed area, and is owned by an organisation that cannot hope to conserve it all? Who can, in fact, only conserve a part by redeveloping the remainder of the site? Conservation Planning is again the most useful framework for managing the process of redevelopment. The writer has spent the last two years co-ordinating a team of archaeologists, historians and ecologists advising such a client on such a site – the Royal Clarence Victualling Yard, Gosport.
   The site's important history, its 15 major historic buildings and structures, its many significant archaeological sites and ecological zones will be reviewed as a means of introducing and discussing the application of the Conservation Plan to the context of a private development.

MANAGEMENT PLANS AND SITE MANAGEMENT OF WORLD HERITAGE SITES
Dr Christopher Young, Head of World Heritage and
 International Policy, English Heritage

The World Heritage Committee requires all cultural World Heritage Sites to 'have ...protection and management mechanisms to ensure the conservation of the nominated cultural properties or cultural landscapes.' The UK govenment policy is to require management plans for all World Heritage Sites in the United Kingdom. It is intended to have plans completed and adopted for all sites by the time of the World Heritage Committee's first Periodic Review of Europe in 2004 and 2005.

Plans now exist or are in preparation for most of the UK sites. Beginning with that for Hadrian's Wall in 1996, the UK has developed a methodology based very much on the Conservation Plan approach pioneered in Australia, but expanded to cover all aspects of a site's management. Central to the Plan is the definition of the site's significance through a thorough understanding of it. Policies are then constructed to protect that significance through achieving the appropriate balance between conservation, access, the interests of the local community and sustainable use of the site for the benefit of that community and the wider public.

It is essential that any such plan is developed through consensus and negotiation among all the stakeholders since it can only be effective if it is adopted by all concerned with it. It is also vital that plans contain effective policies for their implementation.